in an hour

BY JAMES FISHER

SUSAN C. MOORE, SERIES EDITOR

PLAYWRIGHTS in an hour
know the playwright, love the play

IN AN HOUR BOOKS • HANOVER, NEW HAMPSHIRE • INANHOURBOOKS.COM
AN IMPRINT OF SMITH AND KRAUS PUBLISHERS, INC • SMITHANDKRAUS.COM

With grateful thanks to Carl R. Mueller,
whose fascinating introductions to his translations of the Greek and
German playwrights provided inspiration for this series.

Published by In an Hour Books
an imprint of Smith and Kraus, Inc.
177 Lyme Road, Hanover, NH 03755
inanhourbooks.com SmithandKraus.com

Know the playwright, love the play.

In an Hour, In a Minute, and Theater IQ are registered trademarks of
In an Hour Books.

© 2009 by In an Hour Books
All rights reserved
Manufactured in the United States of America
First edition: April 2010
10 9 8 7 6 5 4 3 2 1

Front cover design by Dan Mehling, dmehling@gmail.com
Text design by Kate Mueller, Electric Dragon Productions
Book production by Dede Cummings Design, DCDesign@sover.net

ISBN-13: 978-1-936232-03-1
ISBN-10: 1-936232-03-0
Library of Congress Control Number: 2009943215

CONTENTS

Why Playwrights in an Hour?

Tｈis new series by Smith and Kraus Publishers titled Playwrights in an Hour has a dual purpose for being; one academic, the other general. For the general reader, this volume, as well as the many others in the series, offers in compact form the information needed for a basic understanding and appreciation of the works of each volume's featured playwright. Which is not to say that there don't exist volumes on end devoted to each playwright under consideration. But inasmuch as few are blessed with enough time to read the splendid scholarship that is available, a brief, highly focused accounting of the playwright's life and work is in order.

The central feature of the series, a thirty- to forty-page essay, integrates the playwright into the context of his or her time and place. And the volumes, though written to high standards of academic integrity, are accessible in style and approach to the general reader as well as to the student, and of course to the theater professional and theatergoer.

These books will serve for the brushing up of one's knowledge of a playwright's career, to the benefit of theater work or theatergoing. The Playwrights in an Hour series represents all periods of Western theater: Aeschylus to Shakespeare to Wedekind to Ibsen to Williams to Beckett, and on to the great contemporary playwrights who continue to offer joy and enlightenment to a grateful world.

Carl R. Mueller
School of Theater, Film and Television
Department of Theater
University of California, Los Angeles

Introduction

The name of Arthur Miller has always been synonomous with moral probity and social passion, even during the decades when his artistic reputation was in decline. Although five years have now passed since his death in 2005, one still feels vibrations from his resonant spirit. Miller's courage and conscience have made him an almost heroic figure in contemporary culture. But his artistic reputation seems to rest largely on the four plays excerpted here — *All My Sons* (1941–46), *Death of a Salesman* (1948–49), *A View From the Bridge* (1956), and *The Crucible* (1952–53) — from among the approximately thirty-five that he wrote in his lifetime.

Miller was one of the last American playwrights to believe that his writing could change the world (in my opinion, August Wilson is his legitimate heir). It was a conviction tied to his debatable insistence that the soul of tragedy resided not in the lives of great people but in "the heart of the average man." In a sense, that was a liberal democratic political judgment. But he did not insist on this position throughout his career, partly as a result of historical accident. Miller was born between two great dramatic moments — the pre-war era of political activism and the post-war era of existential absurdity. He reached artistic maturity toward the end of an age when most thinking people believed it essential to take strong stands against social and political injustice, either through engagement in activist art or through commitment to radical causes or both. But it was Miller's misfortune to have arrived on the scene just a few years too late to find true definition in the political struggles of the time.

Earlier radicals found ready-made solutions for social problems in Marx and Stalin. But Miller seemed a little reticent about embracing a single ideology. Thus, as a political animal, he often gave the impression of having arrived at the parade after all the marching was over. He attended communist meetings, but never actually joined the Party. He was accepted into the Federal Theatre the very year that Congress put an end to it. And he was a little too young to get his seaman's papers on that pilot ship of theater radicalism called the Group Theatre. This accident of timing helped him avoid some of the political missteps of activist drama, and its often raw propagandistic disposition. It also left him without a coherent ideological framework with which to structure his political dissent. Attention must surely be paid! But by whom?

Coming of age in the forties, Miller was nonetheless a child of the thirties, deeply influenced by such passionate pioneers as Hallie Flanagan Davis, leader of the Federal Theatre, and by the style of the Group playwrights, most notably Clifford Odets. But perhaps the greatest stylistic influence on his work was that of another celebrated Group member, Elia Kazan, who became Miller's principal director and collaborator, until their well-publicized split when Elia named names in testimony to the House Un-American Activities Committee. If Miller's work appeared to lose some of its vigor after that falling out, part of the reason lies in the loss of the Kazanian influence, though the two men were briefly reunited during the Lincoln Center production of Miller's *After the Fall* (1963–64).

In that play, as in his autobiographical memoir, *Timebends* (1987), Miller very honestly examines his ambivalent attitude toward celebrity — focusing on his brief marriage to Marilyn Monroe. And in a way, during the final years of his career he tried to redeem that momentary fall from grace. His passionate concern for human freedom, ecology, and justice during his term as president of International Pen marked a return to his early belief that literature could function as an instrument of change. Great, good, bad, or indifferent, Arthur Miller's work bears the stamp of a great conscience, as he pays witness to what was worth criticizing in the American character, and what was worth celebrating.

Robert Brustein
Founding Director of the Yale and American Repertory Theatres
Distinguishing Scholar in Residence, Suffolk University

Miller

IN A MINUTE

A snapshot of the playwright's world. From historical events to pop-culture and the literary landscape of the time, this brief list catalogues events that directly or indirectly impacted the playwright's writing. Play citations refer to opening dates.

Miller

HIS WORKS

DRAMATIC AND OTHER FICTIONAL WORKS
PLAYS

No Villain

They Too Arise (based on *No Villain*)

Honors at Dawn (based on *They Too Arise*)

The Grass Still Grows (based on *They Too Arise*)

The Great Disobedience

The Golden Years

Listen My Children (written with Norman Rosten)

The Man Who Had All the Luck

The Half-Bridge

All My Sons

Death of a Salesman

An Enemy of the People (based on Henrik Ibsen's play)

The Crucible

A View from the Bridge

A Memory of Two Mondays

Incident at Vichy

After the Fall

The Price

The Creation of the World and Other Business

The Archbishop's Ceiling

The American Clock

Playing for Time

I Think About You a Great Deal

I Can't Remember Anything (with *Clara*, part of a double bill called *Danger: Memory!*)

Clara (with *I Can't Remember Anything*, part of a double bill called *Danger: Memory!*)

This section presents a complete list of the playwright's works in chronological order by world premiere date.

x

The Last Yankee
The Ride Down Mt. Morgan
Broken Glass
Mr. Peters' Connections
Resurrection Blues
Finishing the Picture

RADIO PLAYS

The Pussycat and the Plumber Who Was a Man
William Ireland's Confession
Jed Chandler Harris
Captain Paul
The Battle of the Ovens
Thunder from the Mountains
I Was Married in Bataan
Toward a Farther Star
The Eagle's Nest
The Four Freedoms
Listen for the Sound of Wings
That They May Win Bernardine
I Love You
Grandpa and the Statue
The Philippines Never Surrendered
The Guardsman (based on Ferenc Molnár's play)
Pride and Prejudice (based on Jane Austen's novel)
Three Men on a Horse (based on George Abbott's and John C. Holm's play)
The Story of Gus
The Reason Why

NOVEL

Focus

FILMS/SCREENPLAYS

The Story of G. I. Joe
The Hook

The Misfits
Everybody Wins
The Crucible

SHORT STORIES

The Misfits
I Don't Need You Anymore
Homely Girl (1992, published in England as *Plain Girl: A Life*, 1995)

TELEVISION PLAYS

Fame
Playing for Time

SHORT PLAYS

Elegy for a Lady (first part of *Two Way Mirror*)
Some Kind of Love Story (second part of *Two Way Mirror*)

NONFICTION WORKS

Situation Normal (1944), on the war correspondence of Ernie Pyle
In Russia (1969), on Russian life, with photographs by Inge Morath
In the Country (1977), on Miller's Connecticut life, with photographs by
      Inge Morath
Chinese Encounters (1979), Miller's travel journal, with photographs by
      Inge Morath
Salesman in Beijing (1984), Miller's experiences directing a 1983 Beijing
      People's Theatre production of *Death of a Salesman*
Timebends: A Life (1987), Miller's autobiography
On Politics and the Art of Acting (2001), on acting and political theater

CHILDREN'S BOOK

Jane's Blanket, with illustrations by Al Parker. New York: Collier-
      Macmillan, 1963.

Onstage with Miller

Introducing Colleagues and Contemporaries of Arthur Miller

 THEATER

Samuel Beckett, Irish playwright

Eric Bentley, English-born American critic

Albert Camus, French playwright

Lee J. Cobb, American actor

Lillian Hellman, American playwright

William Inge, American playwright

Elia Kazan, Turkish-born director

Tennessee Williams, American playwright

 ARTS

Leonard Bernstein, American composer

Dave Brubeck, American jazz pianist

John Cage, American composer

Ella Fitzgerald, American singer

Margot Fonteyn, ballet dancer

Frida Kahlo, Mexican painter

Birgit Nilsson, Swedish opera singer

Dmitri Shostakovich, Russian composer

 FILM

Ingmar Bergman, Swedish film director

Kermit Bloomgarden, American producer

This section lists contemporaries whom the playwright may or may not have known.

Joseph Cotton, American actor
Henry Fonda, American actor
Alfred Hitchcock, English filmmaker
John Huston, American filmmaker
Katherine Hepburn, American actress
Orson Wells, American director

POLITICS/MILITARY

Adolf Eichmann, German Holocaust architect
Indira Gandhi, Indian prime minister
John F. Kennedy, American president
Thurgood Marshall, American Supreme Court justice
Joseph McCarthy, American senator
Rosa Parks, American civil rights activist
Ronald Reagan, American president
Julius and Ethel Rosenberg, executed by the United States for
    passing military secrets to the Soviets

SCIENCE

Rachel Carson, American environmentalist
Jacques Cousteau, French ecologist
John H. Glenn, Jr., American astronaut
Thor Heyerdahl, Norwegian ethnographer and zoologist
C. Everett Koop, American surgeon general
Eugene P. and Howard T. Odum, American ecologists
Jonas Salk, American virologist and inventor of polio vaccine
John Maynard Smith, English biologist

LITERATURE

W. H. Auden, English-born poet
Italo Calvino, Italian writer
Lawrence Ferlinghetti, American poet

Stanley Kunitz, American poet

James A. Michener, American novelist

Ayn Rand, Russian/American novelist

J. D. Salinger, American writer

Studs Terkel, American writer

RELIGION/PHILOSOPHY

Hannah Arendt, German-Jewish political theorist

Daniel Boorstin, American intellectual

Iris Murdoch, Irish-born American philosopher

John Paul II, Polish pope

Thomas Merton, American Trappist monk

Jean-Paul Sartre, French philosopher

Mother Teresa, Albanian missionary

Lionel Trilling, American critic

SPORTS

James J. Braddock, Irish/American boxer

Joe DiMaggio, American baseball player

Joe Louis, American boxer

Satchel Paige, American baseball player

Jackie Robinson, American baseball player

Max Schmeling, German boxer

Ted Williams, American baseball player

Babe Zaharias, American athlete

INDUSTRY/BUSINESS

Bernard Baruch, American financier

George Eastman, American industrialist and inventor

Marshall Field, American retailer

Henry Ford, American auto manufacturer

Jean Paul Getty, American industrialist
William R. Hearst, American publisher
John D. Rockefeller, American financier
David Sarnoff, Belarusian-born American founder of NBC

MILLER

in an
hour

PRELUDE

Arthur Asher Miller is the quintessential sociopolitical American
dramatist of the post–World War II era. He was born October 17,
1915 to a middle-class Jewish-American family in Manhattan, New
York. Miller's father, Isidore, owned a successful women's clothing
manufacturing business. His mother was a homemaker. At the age of
eight, Miller attended his first Broadway play. This experience began
an interest in the stage that would ultimately lead to a singular sixty-
year career as a playwright. Miller was a member of the "Greatest
Generation." He was the dramatist whose plays (from the mid-1940s
to the mid-1950s most particularly) would, in many respects, articulate
his generation's dilemmas. Miller drew his themes more from the experiences of his parents' generation. Within a year of his symbolic
coming-of-age (his 1928 bar mitzvah), the stock market crashed in
October 1929, setting off the Great Depression. This social catastrophe hit the Miller family with particular force. Their comfortable
middle-class existence was shattered when Isidore Miller's business

---

This is the core of the book. The essay places the playwright in the context of his or her world and analyzes the influences and inspirations within that world.

failed. The family moved from Manhattan to Brooklyn, where they resided at 1350 East 3rd Street. For a time, Miller attended James Madison High School, as his family's fortunes were reduced.

As a result of this economic misfortune, Americans rethought their materialistic values. The times also produced a set of themes for Miller. These ultimately became central to his dramatic art. They would be put into words most vividly in his greatest dramatic achievement, the 1949 drama, *Death of a Salesman*. Miller later recounted in his memoir, *Timebends*, that the Depression caused more than economic loss. He noted that the Depression was "a moral catastrophe, a violent revelation of the hypocrisies behind the façade of American society." Miller became convinced that the shattering of a sense of security in the lives of Americans changed their lives. They changed their view of what had previously been seen as the unshakable ideals of American life. Americans, particularly those who had only come to the United States within the last generation or two, had been firm believers in an "American Dream" of economic opportunity and freedom. This dream was to a great extent deeply shaken in the 1930s. Some, including Miller, turned away from an unquestioning belief in capitalism. They moved toward a brand of socialism drawn from Marx. The possibility of a level economic playing field was attractive and drew some to communism. Miller did not go that far. But for much of his life he believed in Marx's theories.

In his finest dramas Miller was most compelled by the dilemmas facing the generation of his parents. The impact of his father's business failure in the Depression would be given voice throughout his career. This was true from his earliest successes, *All My Sons* and *Death of a Salesman*, and as late as *The American Clock*. The influence of the economic and political terrain of the 1930s on Miller's development as an artist was profound. In many ways, Miller expressed his view that "art ought to be of use in changing society." He came of age in a time in which society changed radically, and his theater, born in this crucible of change in the 1930s, would contribute to changes in the post–World War II American society.

FAMILY MATTERS

Observing the financial stresses facing his parents provided Miller with the material for his future work as a dramatist. But the practical issues of his family's financial strains created obstacles for him in reaching that future. Miller spent some time at James Madison High School, where he played on the football team; then he transferred to Abraham Lincoln High School. This was an important development since it was there that his gifts as a writer first won recognition in school publications.

Graduating from Abraham Lincoln in 1933, Miller briefly enrolled at City College in night school. He also worked at an auto-parts company as a warehouse stock clerk. As the only Jew employed there, Miller encountered anti-Semitic attitudes for the first time. This unhappy experience as the target of prejudice would emerge in Miller's plays. He managed eventually to escape the warehouse, and in 1934, Miller was accepted to the University of Michigan. In order to afford his tuition and living expenses, Miller had to work at a variety of menial jobs. Eventually he was able to secure financial support from the National Youth Administration (NYA), a New Deal program. With his own earnings and the NYA support, Miller was able to stay at the University of Michigan. There his writing skills flowered, and he finished his education.

EDUCATION

Miller initially majored in journalism at the University of Michigan. Among his cocurricular activities, he served as a reporter and night editor for the *Michigan Daily*, the university's student newspaper. He studied classical drama and the plays of William Shakespeare, Henrik Ibsen, and Eugene O'Neill. He was particularly taken with the contemporary dramas of Clifford Odets. For many critics, Odets is the obvious precursor of Miller's politically engaged style. Odets was perhaps the predominant dramatic voice of the Depression. He inspired Miller to examine his own responses to this extraordinary era and the experiences of his Jewish-American family within it. Miller's education in dramatic literature included dramatists who, in their own time and place, viewed the stage as having a significant social responsibility to frame the debate over moral, political, and personal issues. This also drew Miller to those experiments with expressionistic techniques to be found in the work of American playwrights such as Eugene O'Neill and Elmer Rice in the generation before Miller. His selective use of these techniques would be a key element in his most significant drama, *Death of a Salesman*.

Along with journalistic pursuits, Miller began to dabble in playwriting. He completed his first work, *No Villain*, which won the Avery Hopwood Award. This encouraged Miller to switch to an English major. Under the guidance of Professor Kenneth Rowe, Miller experimented further with playwriting. He wrote *Honors at Dawn*, another Hopwood Award winner. Miller's *The Grass Still Grows*, another play, won him a $1,200 Theatre Guild National Award during this time.

Miller graduated from the University of Michigan in 1938 with a B.A. degree in English and several completed plays to his credit. That same year, despite an offer to write screenplays for Twentieth Century Fox, Miller signed on to the Federal Theater Project (FTP). This was a New Deal Works Project Administration program aimed at both employing theater professionals and bringing live theater to every corner of the United States. Before his first play could be produced by the FTP, Congress voted it out of existence, concerned that the FTP was a possible hotbed of communist infiltration into American life. This turn of events forced Miller to take a job as a laborer at the Brooklyn Navy Yard. He also earned income writing radio scripts, many of which were performed on CBS's *Columbia Workshop* and *Cavalcade of America* programs. This was a means of generating additional income that he continued well into the mid-1940s.

MARRIAGE

During his time at the University of Michigan, Miller met Mary Slattery, a Catholic girl and the daughter of an insurance salesman. They were married on August 5, 1940. Their union produced two children, Jane Ellen (b. 1944) and Robert (b. 1947). When America entered World War II in December 1941, Miller was exempted from the service. He had had a high school football injury that had damaged a kneecap. On the home front during the war years, the Millers experienced the deprivations that came with rationing. This added another dimension to the profound influence of the Great Depression on Miller's psyche. Miller struggled for economic security through his writing during the war years. He wrote numerous radio scripts for meager sums to support his family. Meanwhile he was aiming for theatrical success with plays he hoped to have produced on Broadway. Many critics, including Christopher Bigsby, stress that the power of Miller's drama emerges from his ability to turn "abstract issues into human dilemmas." It is more likely the case that Miller transformed the human dilemmas of his own life, of family members, and of the society around him into emotional truth and abstract concepts. These were centered around moral responsibility in the face of societal issues beyond individual control.

Miller's marriage to Mary Slattery was a conventional one — but undermined by the stresses of Miller's work. Once he attained success, it was further undermined by the lure of fame and the mounting pressures of maintaining his successful stature.

BROADWAY AND FAILURE

Miller's prodigious output of radio plays (both original plays and literary adaptations) supported his wife and children. Meanwhile he completed *The Man Who Had All the Luck*, which was produced on Broadway in November 1944. Miller's protagonist, David Beeves, mistrusts the good luck that comes his way while observing that his brother seems to have no luck at all. The brother's dream of playing professional baseball, encouraged by their father, is dashed, and the brother's other ventures end in failure. On the other hand, David's business ventures succeed, as does his marriage and the birth of a healthy son. All the while he obsessively fears disaster in all of these areas, even contemplating suicide. In the final analysis, David accepts his good fortune, although the specter of suicide looms as the play ends (Miller had, in fact, ended a novelized form of this play with Beeves's suicide). *The Man Who Had All the Luck*, with its background of dashed hopes drawn from his youth during the Great Depression, won Miller another Theater Guild National Award. Despite critical approval for its theatrical and symbolic elements, the play closed after a mere four performances (plus two previews). The good reviews recognized Miller's skill, but the critics otherwise felt the play and its themes fell short. This commercial failure forced Miller to continue with radio-script writing while he tried his hand at a novel. *Focus* was published in October 1945 with little critical or popular success. The novel dealt with an anti-Semite, Lawrence Newman, who must get glasses. When he begins to wear them, people think he looks like a Jew. He becomes the object of the sort of discrimination and oppression he had visited on others. Over the course of the novel, Newman comes to understand his own behavior and develops an improved attitude toward his fellow humans.

Disheartened by the failures of *The Man Who Had All the Luck* and *Focus*, Miller determined to write one more play before abandoning his literary ambitions. This time, he directed his attention to the intersections of war and commerce. He used the model of Henrik Ibsen's plays to move him toward a more realistic approach than had been the case with *The Man Who Had All the Luck*. His boundless admiration for Ibsen's achievement aided an evolving style. For this, he owed much to the modernist well-made play formula, enhancing the socially conscious themes Miller brought to his next play. For Miller, the Ibsenite model supplied a linear cause-and-effect dramatic structure. In addition, the traditional well-made play provided a template of rising and falling action leading to a climax and denouement. This gave him a firm structure through which to express his themes. The result was a commercial and critical success — and the true beginning of his long playwriting life.

BROADWAY AND SUCCESS

In 1947, Miller's *All My Sons*, in a highly praised production directed by Elia Kazan, opened on Broadway at the Coronet Theater. It ran for 328 performances and won the New York Drama Critics Circle Award, the Donaldson Award, and two Antoinette Perry "Tony" Awards. Writing in *The New York Times*, critic Brooks Atkinson proclaimed that the American theater had "acquired a genuine new talent." The play's drama centers on the Keller family patriarch, Joe Keller. He has attained wealth making airplane components during World War II. Keller had at one time shipped defective parts, leading to the deaths of twenty-one pilots. His arrest causes a son, Larry, who is serving in the military, to commit suicide. This leads Keller to lie and place the blame on his business partner, Steven Deever. Keller is cleared, and Deever is sent to prison. Meanwhile, Kate, Keller's wife, is in deep denial about their son's suicide. She wants to believe that he still lives.

Chris, another Keller son, proposes to Larry's fiancée. This sets off family tensions, leading, finally, to a revelation of Keller's guilt. Chris, who had also served in the military and witnessed many deaths, thoroughly rejects his father on learning of his guilt. Keller, coming to understand his responsibility for Larry's death, kills himself. Critic Harold Bloom views Keller as "an authentic American Everyman" in that he is "an ordinary man who wants to have a moderately good time, who wants his family never to suffer, and who lacks any real imagination beyond the immediate." Bloom is least convinced by the obtuse Keller's arrival at a moral awareness, in the play's climax, that has not been evident in him before. In Miller's drama such moments are essential. They provide the revelation of the moral path and the culpability of those who have strayed from it. Subsequent characters in his major plays, like Keller, face a moral reckoning. As they do, they deliver Miller's notions of moral responsibility, both within a character's personal life and as a citizen of a society.

Miller found his footing as a dramatist with *All My Sons*. He learned that within the tensions of family life he could place the moral considerations of the post–World War II era, which were to be central to his finest works throughout his long and varied career.

Following the failures of his play *The Man Who Had All the Luck*, as well as his novel, *Focus*, Miller's outlook profoundly changed in the wake of *All My Sons*. This is made clear from his statement that it was "somewhat like pushing against a door which is suddenly opened that was always securely shut until then. For myself, the experience was invigorating. It suddenly seemed that the audience was a mass of blood relations, and I sensed a warmth in the world that had not been there before. It made it possible to dream of daring more and risking more." This new daring, as well as Miller's close working relationship with Kazan, were lasting outcomes of *All My Sons*. So also were accusations that Miller was a communist. These resulted, in part, from the play's condemnation of war profiteering among American corporate leaders. It also came from his close relationship with Kazan and others who were similarly branded.

The financial rewards of a successful Broadway run of *All My Sons* liberated Miller to quit radio-script writing. It also gave him the resources to purchase a comfortable home in Roxbury, Connecticut. On his property there, he immediately constructed a small writing studio. Over the course of six weeks in 1948, he wrote his next drama, *Death of a Salesman*, in this studio.

BROADWAY AND TRIUMPH

On February 10, 1949, *Death of a Salesman*, directed by Kazan and with a memorable scenic design by Jo Mielziner, opened at Broadway's Morosco Theatre. It starred Lee J. Cobb as Miller's most iconic character, Willy Loman. Both play and production were widely acclaimed. The play won both the Tony Award as Best Play and the Pulitzer Prize for Drama, among other kudos. It sold in excess of 200,000 copies when it was published. It was also offered by the Book-of-the-Month Club. A 1951 film version, starring Frederic March, was nominated for several Academy Awards and Golden Globes.

As had been the case with *All My Sons*, Miller took his thematic concerns about the underside of the American Dream of materialism into the heart of a troubled family. He melded Ibsenite realism with light expressionistic touches. In the play, aging travelling salesman Willy Loman is unraveling emotionally. Although his supportive wife, Linda, attempts to offer comfort and protect him, Willy's illusions of the economic success he had spent his life striving for are crumbling before him. He can barely make a minimum payment on a refrigerator. Despite Linda's belief that they will get by financially, Willy shows signs of losing his grip. From misplaced eyeglasses to nearly driving off the road, Willy is lost in his own head. He is revisiting in his mind turning points, seeking to know why he has not succeeded in his material goals. In desperation, he turns to his boss, Howard, in hopes that he can get off the road and have a desk job. Instead, this young son of his original employer unsympathetically fires Willy. This sets off a series of illusory flashbacks (although the play's original director, Elia Kazan, referred to these as "daydreams" in which "Willy is justifying himself") in which Willy drifts away. He is lost in significant moments in his past that are muddled with intrusions from the present. Some of Willy's illusions provide comforting happy moments from the past. However, most are critical transitional encounters, including visions of his financially successful older brother, Ben. Ben has carved a fortune out of some far-off adventure. These illusions are distorted. Ben ultimately gives Willy his approval to commit suicide as Willy concocts the misguided notion that his insurance money would provide Biff, Willy's teenage son, with a chance to succeed. This is an unlikely scenario, because Biff will not succeed as Willy imagines. In another flashback, a heartbreaking moment is revealed in which Biff, as an adoring teenager, catches his father in a Boston hotel room with another woman. Biff's dashed illusions about his father poison the young man's life. More particularly, they poison his relationship with Willy. A thinly veiled antagonism grows in Biff. Then, as a grown man, it is clear that he has failed to live up to his potential ("I don't know — what I'm supposed to want," he laments to his brother). Seemingly an unconscious act of aggression against his father, Biff refuses to succeed, which is Willy's dream for him. His success would possibly redeem Willy's own material failure. In flashbacks, we see Willy convincing Biff that the young man is somehow special, too good to be bound by the demands of responsibility others must face. Convinced that Biff can do better, Willy convinces him to see Bill Oliver about a job. Oliver is a businessman Biff worked for as a teenager and from whom he stole. Oliver does not remember Biff, who impulsively steals a gold fountain pen from Oliver's office while alone there. Willy is crushed by the revelation of this self-destructive act. He cannot fully grasp its significance, causing a frustrated Biff to confront him with the truth: "I stole my way out of every good job since high school . . . And I never got anywhere because you blew me so full of hot air I could never stand to take orders from anybody!" Willy's other son, Happy, is also something of a moral reprobate. When the two sons abandon their distressed father in a restaurant, Linda angrily confronts them — "Don't you care whether he lives or dies?" To press her point, she shows them evidence that Willy has been contemplating suicide. The sons come to realize that Willy has not been true to himself. He has always enjoyed working with his hands, but the idea of being a carpenter falls short of Willy's illusion of the American Dream. Estranged from his sons and a failure as a salesman, Willy misguidedly commits suicide to provide insurance money to help Biff attain success ("I've got nothing to give him," he laments throughout the play). However, at his graveside, Linda and the sons know that Willy's act was futile. The insurance company will not pay a benefit for a suicide.

Kazan saw Willy's tragedy as a modern-day conundrum in which the individual "is Always Anxious! Because he is between two opposite fatal pulls: to best his neighbor, his brother vs. to be loved by his brother. These are mutually exclusive, an impossible contradiction. Inevitably it will end disastrously," as, of course, it does for Willy.

Kazan also gravitated toward the expressionistic aspects of the play. For all characters but the Lomans, Miller merely supplied first names ("Charley," "Bernard," "Howard") and for minor characters, no name at all ("The Woman"). Thus he made certain that despite the play's realistic aspects, these characters become no more than representative types.

Kazan was greatly aided by Jo Mielziner's now famous scene design for the play. This featured a skeletal outline of the Loman house, with the roof bowing down as if the weight of the surrounding large apartment houses is slowly crushing it. The house was about to implode, just as Willy himself does. Mielziner's fragmented design featured a few sketched-in outlines of its structure mixed with a few levels and selected pieces of furniture. This allowed the actors to move easily from present to past in Willy's daydreams. It also underscored the similarly sketchy, fragile barrier between reality and illusion in Willy's troubled mind.

The triumph of *Death of a Salesman* was remarkable on several counts. Not least is its depiction of the dark side of capitalism — or, at least, the illusions it can create in those who view material success as fulfillment (the vaunted "American Dream"). This was in stark contrast to America's post–World War II economic boom. In every respect, *Death of a Salesman* seemed to counter the contemporary currents of American life. Although on the surface more a play about the Great Depression of the 1930s, *Death of a Salesman* still managed to speak to its audience in 1949, perhaps as a cautionary tale. This grim drama, ending with its protagonist's futile suicide, received glowing reviews. It ran until November 1950, racking up an impressive 742 performances. More importantly, the extraordinary critical acclaim it received placed it within the pantheon of the greatest American plays. In the subsequent sixty years since its premiere, *Death of a Salesman* has had numerous revivals. Its also been featured in film and television productions, and it has had a healthy life in print. Often at the top of listings of "greatest American plays," *Death of a Salesman* won Miller a rarified place with Eugene O'Neill and Tennessee Williams as part of a triumvirate of America's greatest playwrights.

INFLUENCES

Critics have identified a range of literary and theatrical influences in Miller's work, and many of these are particularly evident in *All My Sons* and *Death of a Salesman*. Miller himself directed his audience and critics to classical tragedy as a central influence on his work in the wake of *Death of a Salesman*. He posited in the essay "Tragedy and the Common Man" that the model of ancient tragedy, especially the works of Sophocles, had inspired him. The essay appeared in *The New York Times*. He also wrote that "the tragic feeling is evoked in us when we are in the presence of a character who is ready to lay down his life, if need be, to secure one thing — his sense of personal dignity." Miller implanted this struggle in Willy Loman, an ordinary man at the end of his rope. Unable even to make a minimal payment on his refrigerator, having lost the respect of his favored son, and losing the job to which he has devoted his life (and the dream of material success he has clung to), Willy's psyche unravels. He drifts between significant past events and his distressed present. Without achieving financial success, Willy finds his life to be empty. His dreams are shattered, his self-esteem is in tatters. In this, Miller places Willy among the great characters of the tragic tradition. He noted that from "Orestes to Hamlet, Medea to

Macbeth, the underlying struggle is that of the individual attempting to gain his 'rightful' position in society." Willy's failure to do so is, in this sense, the heart of his tragedy, despite his "commonness." For Miller, Willy is "as apt a subject for tragedy in its highest sense as kings were." Some critics disagreed, finding Willy's travails too ordinary to rise to the level of tragedy in the classical sense.

Willy is, at the least, an American tragic hero. He is a representative of a certain set of American values drawn from the well of consumerism and conformity. He admires brand-name products. He spouts advertising slogans in one breath, while cursing the machines in the next breath when they fail to function properly. Biff's success in high school sports is highly prized by Willy. Willy has based his sense of dignity entirely on societally approved modes of success. These might be the attainment of brand-name appliances or his son's predominance on the playing field. His profession as a salesman, the sort of individual who makes his way in the world with nothing more than "a smile and a shoeshine," is in itself an embodiment of the American values Willy worships. Yet he finds that these values bring him neither material nor personal fulfillment

Willy's illusion of his worth is shattered when it becomes clear that he has failed to achieve financial success. This is brought into full focus when he is fired from his job. There is nothing left to sustain him — it is a humiliation too great to bear. This becomes clear when Willy's kindly neighbor, Charley, offers a loan. Willy cannot tolerate this or see it as an act of kindness. In his eyes, it is a condemnation. He has failed, and that is his ultimate tragedy in his own eyes.

Miller intends for the audience to see Willy's self-delusion and misguided values as the basis of his true tragedy. He understood that a revival of tragedy in the modern theater must significantly depart from at least one aspect of its ancient tradition — its protagonist must be an ordinary individual. For Miller, those exalted figures at the center of Greek drama who fall from great heights through hubris or some other fundamental weakness were no longer appropriate tragic figures. In a modern tragedy, a Willy Loman is the appropriate protagonist, an individual whose weakness is his failure to recognize his true nature. Willy has placed his faith in false materialistic values and in various forms of self-delusion. He has worshipped a false god, but his failure is his rejection of his true nature. Willy's tragedy is not a fall from a great height. His tragedy is in failing to know himself. Miller concluded in "Tragedy and the Common Man" that it is "time that we, who are without kings, took up this bright thread of our history and followed it to the only place it can possibly lead in our time — the heart and spirit of the average man."

Other influences in Miller's work may be found closer to his own time. He admired America's foremost dramatist, Eugene O'Neill. In addition, the associations between Miller's work and that of 1930s leftist playwright Clifford Odets (and The Group Theatre, the firebrand company that produced Odets's greatest works) are unmistakable. However, the modern playwright most responsible for Miller's earliest successful works was Henrik Ibsen. In 1936, at the beginning of his playwriting career, Miller attended a performance of a Broadway revival of Ibsen's *A Doll's House*. He was profoundly moved by the play and by actress Ruth Gordon's performance as Nora Helmer, Ibsen's protagonist. This experience ignited Miller's lifelong admiration for Ibsen's dramatic goals and style. In 1950, following on the acclaim for *Death of a Salesman*, Miller completed a modern adaptation of Ibsen's *An Enemy of the People*. It starred Frederic March and Florence Eldridge. Miller's respect for Ibsen was such that his adaptation is faithful to the original in the extreme. Dr. Stockmann, the play's protagonist, finds himself at odds with his resort-town community when he refuses to conceal information about dangers in the local waters, thus damaging the town's economic fortunes. Stockmann's embrace of moral responsibility for others was obviously what attracted Miller to this particular play of Ibsen's. It was a recurrent thread in Miller's plays. Despite the acting of March and Eldridge, and the cachet of Miller's involvement on the heels of the triumph of *Death of a Salesman*, *An*

Enemy of the People eked out a mere thirty-six performances. But later Miller's adaptation was used for a 1977 film adaptation featuring actor Steve McQueen. Among the themes of *An Enemy of the People*, Miller emphasized the struggle of an individual against the corrupted values of a society placing economic security over truth. Miller's attraction to such a dilemma would emerge in his next major dramatic work — and he would find himself in a similar situation.

CITIZEN AND ACTIVIST

Elia Kazan had directed *Death of a Salesman* and worked with Miller on an unproduced screenplay called *The Hook*. In 1952, Kazan appeared before the House Un-American Activities Committee (HUAC). Fearful of being blacklisted by Hollywood, he identified eight people from the Group Theatre as members of the Communist Party. Kazan had been a key member of the Group Theatre during the 1930s. They had espoused a socialist doctrine in response to the apparent failure of capitalism in the midst of the Great Depression. However, after the onset of the Cold War In the forties, members of such left-leaning organizations drew the attention of HUAC.

Miller returned from Hollywood, where he had been unsuccessful in finding a producer interested in filming *The Hook*, and where he had met actress Marilyn Monroe. He was initially shocked by Kazan's co-operation with HUAC. He explains this in his autobiography, *Timebends*.

> Listening to him I grew frightened. There was a certain gloomy logic in what he was saying: unless he came clean he could never hope, in the height of his creative powers, to make another film in America, and he would probably not be given a passport to work abroad either. If the theatre remained open to him, it was not his primary interest anymore; he wanted to deepen his film life, that was where his heart lay, and he had been told in so many words by his old boss

and friend Spyros Skouras, president of Twentieth Century Fox, that the company would not employ him unless he satisfied the Committee.

> . . . unbelievable as it seemed, I could still be up for sacrifice if Kazan knew I attended meetings of the Communist Party writers years ago and had made a speech at one of them.

In *Timebends*, Miller also discussed the impact of the HUAC blacklist on his friend Louis Untermeyer. Then Miller talks about the HUAC involvement of Lee J. Cobb. Cobb was the first actor to play Willy Loman in *Death of a Salesman* on Broadway. After Miller's meeting with Kazan, the two men did not speak again for ten years.

Preparing for his next play, Miller spent time in Salem, Massachusetts, where in 1692 several individuals had been tried for witchcraft and executed. Poring over the records of the witch trials, Miller recognized a parallel with current events. He set about crafting *The Crucible*, a historical drama about the witch trials with obvious allegorical undercurrents.

Drawing on names and incidents in the historical record of Salem at the time of the witch trials, Miller crafts a drama of John Proctor, a farmer who is dragged into the trials by the accusations of several young girls caught dancing in the nearby woods. Proctor has had a brief affair with Abby Putnam, the ringleader of the accusers. John goes to the gallows when his wife, Elizabeth, lies about the affair to save John's name. The authorities offer John the opportunity of saving himself by admitting to witchcraft and by naming others. He refuses to betray his friends and neighbors. The connections to the "witch hunt" of Miller's own day are clear. His emphasis on John's honorable resistance to saving himself by selling out others vividly illustrates his feelings about those witnesses, like Kazan, who cooperated with HUAC's insistence and named others.

The Crucible opened at the Martin Beck Theatre on January 22, 1953. The response of critics and audiences was tepid, with the contemporary echoes generating controversy. The play closed after 197 performances. It is now considered one of Miller's finest works. This play has frequently been revived on Broadway — in 1964, 1972, 1991, and 2002. It has been filmed twice. It was adapted in French by Jean-Paul Sartre in 1957. It was also produced as a major Hollywood film in 1996, starring Winona Ryder and Daniel Day-Lewis, Miller's son-in-law.

The Crucible, and the controversy surrounding it, attracted the attention of HUAC. The committee denied Miller a passport when he planned to attend the play's 1954 London premiere. Kazan felt the sting of *The Crucible*. He responded with his film *On the Waterfront* (1954), which featured a heroic dockworker who testifies against a crooked union boss despite facing violence. The dockworker was played by Marlon Brando in an Academy Award–winning performance.

Miller's response to Kazan's self-justifying film came in the form of his next major play, *A View from the Bridge*. It was originally a long one-act play presented on a double bill with Miller's *A Memory of Two Mondays*. *A Memory of Two Mondays* was set during the Depression. It examines the economic fears and prejudices of characters based on those whom Miller worked with in an auto-parts warehouse during his youth. The anger Miller felt toward the anti-Semites he faced there is presented, though tempered by his compassion for those who, unlike him, could not escape the deprivations and struggles he ultimately escaped.

In *A View from the Bridge*, Miller turns the tables on Kazan's *On the Waterfront*. He depicts a dockworker who informs on two illegal immigrants for personal gain. The story of the central character, Eddie Carbone, is recounted by a lawyer, Alfieri. Living in a blue-collar, Italian-American neighborhood, Eddie has helped to raise the niece of his wife, Beatrice. The girl, Catherine, has grown into a lovely young woman. Eddie experiences unarticulated sexual feelings for her. These come to the fore when Beatrice's cousins, Rodolpho and Marco, arrive in New York as illegal immigrants. Eddie is jealous of Catherine's attraction to Rodolpho. Eddie tries to warn Catherine away from the young man. He even goes so far as to suggest that Rodolpho is gay. In desperation, Eddie defies the code of his neighborhood and reports Marco to the immigration authorities. Marco vows revenge and confronts Eddie, who draws a knife. In the ensuing struggle, Eddie is killed with his own knife. Like Willy Loman in *Death of a Salesman*, Eddie fails to understand himself and his motives. Again, it is Eddie's role as an informant that drives the play. For Miller, Eddie's unforgivable act is betraying those who trusted him. Like *The Crucible*, *A View from the Bridge*'s initial lukewarm critical response has been replaced with admiration and frequent revivals.

The Crucible and *A View from the Bridge* belong to a period in which Miller's personal and political experiences merged. As such, they may be viewed as the pinnacle of Miller's political drama as his attention shifted to changes in his personal life that would refocus his drama.

MARILYN MONROE

As acclaim for Miller's playwriting grew, his personal life went through a radical change. This may have begun with a brief affair he had with film actress Marilyn Monroe during a Hollywood visit in 1951. Miller and Monroe had remained in contact during her marriage to baseball legend Joe DiMaggio. When that marriage ended, and despite his own marriage, Miller and Monroe reunited. Miller travelled to Nevada for a divorce from his wife in June 1956. This trip also inspired his subsequent screenplay *The Misfits*. Almost immediately after, on June 29, 1956, Miller and Monroe married. Monroe converted to Judaism to please Miller. Their marriage set off a major media frenzy.

Miller's high-profile marriage to Monroe had one unintended effect. HUAC almost immediately served him with a subpoena, demanding his appearance before the committee. This was an obvious attempt to draw media attention to HUAC's hearings. Miller only agreed to appear if HUAC's chairman would agree not to force him to name names. Testifying before the committee, Miller, accompanied by Monroe, admitted to attending Communist Party meetings in the 1940s. Not long after this appearance, Miller travelled to England, where Monroe was to appear in the film *The Prince and the Showgirl*, co-starring with Laurence Olivier. In a turnabout, HUAC changed its mind about "naming names." HUAC succeeded in getting a federal district court to convict Miller of contempt of Congress. As a result, Miller was given a one-month suspended sentence and fined $500. Insisting "I could not use the name of another person and bring trouble on him," Miller was unrepentant. This caused him to be blacklisted, and again his passport was withdrawn. However, Miller won ultimate vindication. In 1958, his conviction was overturned when the court of appeals was convinced that Miller had been misled by HUAC's chairman.

As a result of this battle, and Miller's rocky marriage to Monroe, his work as a dramatist was severely undermined. The ups and downs caused by Monroe's addictions and the demands of her screen career superseded Miller's work. He attempted to meld the two by writing a film, *The Misfits*, as a gift for Monroe. Under the direction of John Huston, *The Misfits* went before the cameras in Nevada in 1960. It starred Marilyn Monroe, Clark Gable, Montgomery Clift, and Eli Wallach. It proved to be a troubled shoot mostly due to Monroe's erratic behavior, which severely damaged her relationship with Miller.

In Miller's screenplay, Gay, Perce, and Guido are three present-day cowboys who, in their individual ways, have failed to adjust to changing times. They drink, chase women, and behave with reckless abandon in a world they believe neither understands them nor respects their values and traditions. After a harrowing chase of wild mustangs, Gay, one of the cowboys, is profoundly influenced by Roslyn. She is a divorced young woman, who both urges him to let the mustangs run free and shows him the way to a new and different life.

When *The Misfits* was completed, Miller and Monroe divorced in January 1961. This was a month before the premiere of *The Misfits*, which was generally well received by critics and popular with the public. The film had a tragic element — Gable died suddenly of a heart attack shortly after the completion of filming. Unfortunately, although she began work on a subsequent film, *The Misfits* proved to be Monroe's final completed work. She committed suicide in August 1962.

Miller remarried not long after his divorce from Monroe. He had met photographer Inge Morath, and they wed on February 17, 1962. Their union produced two children, Rebecca (b. 1962) and Daniel (b. 1966). Daniel was born with Down's syndrome. At Miller's insistence and declining to resist the practices of the time, the child was institutionalized. Miller rarely saw the boy, although through the efforts of Rebecca's husband, Daniel Day-Lewis, near the end of his life Miller spent time with his son. The marriage to Morath was enduring, lasting until her death in 2002.

THE SIXTIES AND BEYOND

Miller's next major play, *After the Fall*, brought together myriad strands of his professional and personal life. Despite the chill in their relationship from the HUAC days, Miller reunited with director Elia Kazan. In 1964 they worked together again on the production, which was staged by Kazan at the ANTA Theatre as the inaugural production of the Lincoln Center Repertory Theater. *After the Fall* opened on January 23, 1964. Although Miller tended to downplay the autobiographical elements, it was clear to critics and audiences that the play was a dramatization of Miller's experiences married to Monroe.

In *After the Fall*, Miller returned to the topic of betrayal, both personal and public. His protagonist, Quentin, a lawyer, in an elaborate monologue, revisits his relationships with various women in his life. These include his mother and his two wives, one of whom is a drug-addled, emotionally unstable actress. Quentin has been profoundly altered by his experiences, including the Great Depression, the Holocaust, and the HUAC hearings. He has married again and contemplates the possibility of finding happiness.

The premiere of *After the Fall* so soon after Monroe's tragic death set off a media firestorm. The press accused Miller of unseemly self-justification and exploitation of Monroe's memory. Critics were almost uniformly negative. They were more appreciative of Miller's *Incident at Vichy*, also produced by the Lincoln Center Repertory Theater. All in all, the early 1960s proved to be frustrating in regard to his playwriting, although his political interests filled the void.

Incident at Vichy had been inspired, to a great extent, by Miller's temporary assignment as a reporter for the *New York Herald-Tribune*. He covered war trials of Nazi SS officers in Frankfurt, Germany, in February 1964. Conceived as a companion piece to *After the Fall*, *Incident at Vichy* explored anti-Semitic attitudes that, in Miller's estimation, led to the horrors of the Holocaust. Several prisoners from different walks of life are detained in Vichy, France, at the start of the Nazi occupation in 1942. Awaiting interrogation, the prisoners debate issues of the occupation. They discuss issues from anti-Semitism to the growing resistance movement. Among the prisoners, a non-Jewish prince establishes the meaning of resistance by trading his life for that of a Jewish prisoner, Leduc. The gesture becomes an eloquent statement of the purpose of resistance and gives meaning to the sacrifice.

In the year following *Incident at Vichy*, Miller became president of PEN (Poets, Playwrights, Essayists, and Novelists). This group of politically engaged writers supports freedom of speech and freedom from oppression for international writers. Miller travelled to Poland and the Soviet Union on PEN's behalf. He is credited with helping dissident playwrights Wole Soyinka and Fernando Arrabal. By 1969, the Soviet Union banned Miller's work, largely due to his work with PEN.

In this period, Miller was drawn to the case of Peter Reilly, a young man in Miller's home state of Connecticut accused of murdering his mother. Miller raised funds for a detective and lawyer for the boy. After expert witnesses were able to undermine the case against Reilly, he was freed in 1976. Miller's experience with this case led to his screenplay *Everybody Wins* (1990). It starred Nick Nolte and Debra Winger, but the film failed to win critical approval.

Back in the United States, Miller participated in protests against America's involvement in the Vietnam War as it escalated throughout the decade of the 1960s. Miller had not presented a new play since *After the Fall* and *Incident at Vichy* in 1964. On February 7, 1968, his new work, *The Price*, opened at the Morosco Theatre on Broadway. It ran for an impressive 429 performances. This was his most commercially successful work since *Death of a Salesman*. *The Price* won Miller a Tony Award as Best Play. It also garnered some much-needed critical approval after the devastating response to *After the Fall*.

The Price is a penetrating family drama. It offers echoes of *Death of a Salesman* in that its two lately estranged middle-aged brothers, Victor and Walter Franz, seem in many respects to be merely older extensions of *Death of a Salesman's* two brothers, Biff and Happy. Thematically, *The Price* stresses sibling dynamics and the personal and moral decisions the individual makes. To provide a metaphorical background for the choices made by the brothers, Miller adds an elderly Jewish furniture dealer, Gregory Solomon. He joins the brothers in the attic of their late father's home to dicker over the price of the remaining pieces of furniture that belonged to the elder Franz. The deep familial resentments between the two brothers are set against ruefully humorous elements introduced by Solomon. Victor is a poorly paid policeman, Walter a respected surgeon. Solomon provides perspective on the inability of the brothers to understand themselves and their relationship. The introduction of centrally comic elements in Miller's work would be reflected in some of his subsequent plays. *The Price* gains its strength from a revisiting of both the style and themes of *All My Sons* and *Death of a Salesman*.

LATER WORKS

Miller's dramatic output continued throughout the 1970s until his death. Critical and commercial success were elusive. In part, this was true because Miller occasionally moved away from the realistic style typical of his most acclaimed dramas, *All My Sons*, *Death of a Salesman*, *The Crucible*, *A View from the Bridge*, and *The Price*. After his marriage to Inge Morath, Miller spent more time travelling. He collaborated with her on the books *In the Country* and *Chinese Encounter* by contributing texts in support of Morath's photographs. Miller also completed a few one-act plays and short stories, most notably *Fame* and *The Reason Why*. He ultimately expanded *Fame* into a 1978 screenplay with the same name. It features a successful playwright's struggles to accept his fame and its costs, particularly to those around him. As with *The Misfits*, a woman leads the playwright to a vision of a different life and to valuing what he possesses. With a strong cast including Richard Benjamin, José Ferrer, Raf Vallone, and Linda Hunt, *Fame* was broadcast in late 1978 on NBC-TV's *Hallmark Hall of Fame* as a one-hour film. It met predominantly with critical approval.

Miller's next major play, *The Creation of the World and Other Business*, did not fare as well. It proved to be a true departure from Miller's earlier Ibsen-inspired realistic style. This highly theatrical comedy was inspired by the early chapters of the Book of Genesis. It presents God as a good, but buffoonish, figure unable to control the behavior of his creations. Lucifer, an articulate figure, posits that evil must exist for good to be fully appreciated. This notion is demonstrated in episodes depicting Adam and Eve, Cain and Abel, and other Biblical figures. The emphasis on the struggle of good and evil is the only element in *The Creation of the World and Other Business* that could be said to be typical of Miller. Otherwise, the play is unlike his prior work. As such, it confused critics and audiences despite being marketed as a comedy. It opened at Broadway's Shubert Theatre on November 30, 1972, with a stellar cast including Zöe Caldwell, George Grizzard, and Bob Dishy. It garnered mixed to negative reviews, and folded after a mere twenty performances (and twenty-one previews). The play was subsequently reworked as a musical, *Up from Paradise*. Unfortunately, it received no greater critical or commercial appreciation.

Miller's next few plays fared no better than *The Creation of the World and Other Business*. *The Archbishop's Ceiling*, a 1977 drama set in Czechoslovakia, created an illusion that Miller was returning to the realistic, Ibsenite style that had marked his earlier works, although the play's subject, in part, deals with an exploration of the means of dramatic expression. The plot centers around an American writer, Adrian, who experiences life behind the Iron Curtain through the experiences of Sigmund, a dissident writer. Sigmund must make a grim choice between saving his life or his work. Adrian and his friends, including a former mistress, help Sigmund save a recently completed manuscript that has been confiscated by the government. As Enoch Brater writes in *Arthur Miller's America: Theater and Culture in a Time of Change*, Miller repudiates the "dramatic form he had earlier championed." He signaled this change through "the play's shift from stage technology to poetic trope; in other words, from theatrical devices that drive the plot forward, as in Ibsen, to a single metaphor." In this case "the bugged ceiling of the mind," as Miller describes his central character's dilemma. This dilemma is reflected in the play's setting, a study formerly belonging to an archbishop. The study may, in fact, be literally "bugged" as a means of political oppression within what Brater describes as the play's "superficially conventional plot." The character's state of mind and the literal bugging of the room reflect the play's ideas on political oppression. Miller's experimentation did not sit well with the critics: *The Archbishop's Ceiling* did not find favor.

Miller's next play also failed to find approval. *The American Clock* (subtitled *A Mural for the Theatre*) was a sweeping drama of the Great Depression. It was set within the context of a family not unlike his own. It offered a cross-section of various experiences of the era — both those who survived and those who were crushed by it. The play offers images of both successful and failed businessmen, intellectuals, farmers, and others. It focuses on the Baum family. Moe, the father, suffers business reversals. He continues in his work, even as his wife, Rose, cannot bear up under the economic strains and attendant fears. Their son, Lee, grows from youth to adulthood travelling the nation. Ultimately, he comes to terms with its wonders and failings. The autobiographical elements in Miller's depiction of the Baum family are unmistakable. They were enhanced in the original production by the fact that Miller's sister, Joan Copeland, played Rose. This character was based on their mother, Augusta Miller. The original production of *The American Clock* opened at New York's Biltmore Theatre on November 20, 1980, following a run at the Spoleto Festival in Charleston, South Carolina. The Broadway production closed after a mere twelve performances (and eleven previews). This was a shattering commercial failure despite respectful reviews and a Drama Desk Best Actress Award for Joan Copeland.

This failure came only weeks after Miller's teleplay, *Playing for Time*, had been broadcast to critical acclaim on CBS-TV on September 30, 1980. *Playing for Time* was adapted from the memoirs of Fania Fénelon, a Jewish woman prisoner at Auschwitz death camp during World War II. She, along with other prisoners, was spared from death to form a camp orchestra. It features the notorious Dr. Josef Mengele as a secondary character. However, Miller reserves his attention for the interactions of Jewish and non-Jewish musicians who are willing or unwilling to participate in the orchestra. They provide Fénelon with lessons on surviving the horrors surrounding her. Controversy centered on the casting of Vanessa Redgrave as Fénelon due to Redgrave's outspoken support of the Palestinians. The real Fénelon spoke out against the casting of Redgrave. Despite this, Redgrave retained the role. She won an Emmy Award for her performance (as did her co-star Jane Alexander). *Playing for Time* won a prestigious Peabody Award for television excellence.

Miller's *Two-Way Mirror* consists of two works, *Elegy for a Lady* and *Some Kind of Love Story*. It was completed between 1982 and 1984.

In *Elegy for a Lady*, a man enters a boutique seeking a gift for his lover, who is ill. While discussing gift options with the store's owner, the man explores his relationship with his lover and his own actions. *Some Kind of Love Story* presents a private detective questioning a woman with a multiple-personality disorder who is a potential witness in a case. It soon becomes clear that the detective and the woman are locked into a continuing loop that may never lead to the answers the detective seeks. Miller's 1987 *Danger: Memory!* explored similar terrain. It also consisted of two one-acts, *I Can't Remember Anything* and *Clara*. In the first, *I Can't Remember Anything*, two old friends, Leonora and Leo, debate their relationship and divergent views of life in the wake of the death of Leonora's husband. *Clara* pits a detective against the father of a murdered woman. This reveals more about the father than the victim. These plays failed to spark much interest, and new Miller plays were a rarity by the early 1980s.

In 1983, Miller returned to *Death of a Salesman* when he travelled to the People's Republic of China to direct its first production there, in Beijing. The play was well received. A year later Miller published his account of the experience in *Salesman in Beijing*. In it he chronicled the cultural intersections unearthed by the encounter between this quintessentially American play and a Communist nation largely cut off from the West. *Death of a Salesman* also brought more acclaim to Miller in frequent revivals. In a 1975 Circle in the Square production, George C. Scott won a Tony Award for his acting. He also directed the play. Then a 1984 revival starring Dustin Hoffman won a Tony Award as Best Reproduction of a Play, as well as several Drama Desk Awards. In 1999, another Broadway revival also won a Best-Reproduction-of-a-Play Tony Award. The revival featured Brian Dennehy as Willy Loman. It won several other awards for cast members and the production's director, Robert Falls. The 1984 stage revival inspired a television film version also starring Hoffman. It was first broadcast on CBS-TV on September 15, 1985. (A previous 1966 television film version featured the original Broadway leads, Lee J.

Cobb and Mildred Dunnock.) This film drew an estimated 25 million viewers. It received numerous Emmy and Golden Globe Award nominations and wins.

That same year, Miller was the recipient of a Kennedy Center Honors Lifetime Achievement Award. The *Death of a Salesman* revival, coupled with the publication of *Timebends* (1987), Miller's autobiography, and a revival of interest in his plays in the United States and particularly in Great Britain, seems to have revitalized Miller's interest in playwriting during the last fifteen years of his life. In 1991, Miller's *The Ride Down Mt. Morgan* debuted in London. Nevertheless, it took nearly a decade before the play opened at Broadway's Ambassador Theatre on April 9, 2000, for a 121-performance run. It earned Tony Award and Drama Desk nominations as Best Play. The play is set in a hospital room where Lyman Felt is recovering from a near-fatal auto accident. The situation reveals Lyman's secret. He is a bigamist, and his two wives, previously unaware of each other's existence, meet at his bedside. Confronted with this, Lyman is unable to acknowledge that he has done anything inappropriate, although his daughter and a friend attempt to convince him otherwise. When they fail, all leave him. *The Ride Down Mt. Morgan* finds Miller once again confronting the dilemmas of personal and public betrayal and the absurdity of moral relativism.

Another Miller play, *The Last Yankee*, had both London and New York productions in 1992. Two couples, the Hamiltons and the Fricks, are at a state mental facility where the wives are both in treatment with problems resulting from their marriages. Over the course of the play, Patricia Hamilton faces the fact that her problems stem from too-high expectations of her carpenter husband (who happens to be a descendant of Alexander Hamilton), and they are reconciled. However, the Fricks are unable to work out their issues. *The Last Yankee* was moderately well received. But to some critics it seemed to be a lukewarm rehashing of prior Miller plays. That same year, Miller published *Homely Girl: A Life and Other Stories*. The "other stories" were Miller's previously published

Fame and *Fitter's Night*. *Homely Girl*, a new story, depicted Janice Sessions, a married socialist who finds both her politics and her marriage wanting. She ultimately finds happiness with a blind man. Like *The Last Yankee*, critics were largely unimpressed.

Miller's next play, *Broken Glass*, won considerably more approval. This included a Tony Award nomination as Best Play when it opened on April 24, 1994. It ran for seventy-three performances at New York's Booth Theatre, starring Amy Irving. Irving played Sylvia Gellburg, who suddenly falls ill with a strange paralysis after she sees images of the events of Kristallnacht in the newspaper. Her husband, Philip, the only Jewish employee of a bank, has spent his life trying to assimilate. Sylvia struggles to express her pent-up fears and longings. She is treated by Dr. Harry Hyman, whose own problems are revealed as he attempts to treat Sylvia. This drama, in part, explores the place of Jews in a society in the aftermath of the Holocaust. It offers another attempt by Miller to come to dramatic terms with the Nazi atrocities against Jews. As in the case of Sylvia, even decades after the fact, she is profoundly affected by the Holocaust. Her husband's assimilationist views suggest that these two people are strangers to each other's fears.

Despite its comparatively short Broadway run, *Broken Glass* mostly won admiration from critics, who regarded it as the finest work of Miller's later years. In the mid-1990s, as Miller became an octogenarian, he took on the task of adapting his play *The Crucible* for a 1996 film version produced by his daughter, Rebecca. It starred Miller's son-in-law, Daniel Day-Lewis; Winona Ryder; Joan Allen; and Paul Scofield. This lavish production won much critical acclaim, not to mention an Academy Award nomination for Miller's screenplay.

Miller's seriocomic fantasy, *Mr. Peters' Connections*, opened Off-Broadway on April 28, 1998. It was a production of the Signature Theatre Company, for which he wrote the play, with a stellar cast including Peter Falk and Anne Jackson. The play depicts an old man who visits his brother's rundown nightclub, where he is surprised to encounter family and friends from his past and present. In attempting to make sense of his life, Mr. Peters finds strength to move forward from his daughter's plea that he live. Critics were not kind, with *The New York Times* reviewer Ben Brantley finding it a "numbing experience" and "clumsy." He also felt Miller's "experimental, ruminative style" proved ineffective.

In 2002, Miller received Spain's Principe de Asturias Prize for Literature as "the undisputed master of modern drama." He also won the Jerusalem Prize in 2003. These acknowledgments were marred by the death from cancer of Miller's wife, Inge Morath, in late 2002. Miller pressed on with his writing. He completed *Resurrection Blues*, a satiric play about a television network purchasing the rights to the crucifixion of a South American rebel and purported messiah. This play, which stressed recurring Miller themes on the dangers of blind belief in possibly faulty values, was staged at the Guthrie Theatre in Minneapolis, Minnesota, in 2002. It was followed by a 2006 production staged by Kevin Spacey at London's Old Vic. Miller's final work, *Finishing the Picture*, is a semi-autobiographical poetic comedy dealing with the travails of filming *The Misfits* in 1960 with his troubled ex-wife, Marilyn Monroe. It premiered at Chicago's Goodman Theatre in late 2004. This was shortly before Miller announced he would marry Agnes Barley. She was a thirty-four-year-old painter who had taken up residency on his Roxbury, Connecticut property in 2002, much to the distress of Miller's daughter, Rebecca. When Miller died of congestive heart failure on February 10, 2005, she ordered Barley to vacate the property.

LEGACY

Miller's death, which occurred on the fifty-sixth anniversary of the premiere of *Death of a Salesman* on Broadway, ended an era of American drama. Miller was the last of the "Big Three" titans which included Eugene O'Neill and Tennessee Williams. He was also the American theater's foremost dramatist of social consciousness. Many politically engaged playwrights of subsequent generations, from David Mamet to

Tony Kushner, are in his lasting debt. In March 2007, Miller's alma mater, the University of Michigan, dedicated the Arthur Miller Theatre on its campus. This honored his wish that it be the only theater to bear his name.

Miller's thematic legacy is irrevocably tied to twentieth-century American history, first in the crucible of the Great Depression. The Depression provided the background for many of his finest works, and it was profoundly woven into the texture of his own life. His moral and political foundations were formed in the context of his family's struggles in the 1930s, and in his own experience of anti-Semitism as a young man. This was further fueled by the Holocaust and its aftermath. Then he experienced the war crimes trials, where he observed the perpetrators of the deaths of millions of Jews brought to justice. As a writer, Miller resisted any form of persecution or oppression. Oppression was another topic frequently explored in his dramatic work and a central part of his political activism.

In the decade following World War II, Miller reached his zenith as a playwright. His greatest play, *Death of a Salesman*, although set in present-day 1949, is more truly a play of the 1930s. It was burnished by the Depression and, ultimately, by the war years. His exploration of the bleak aspects of American capitalism was depicted in Willy Loman's material failure. This made Miller himself the target of political oppression in the early 1950s. It inspired him to depict the notorious Salem witch trials of 1692. He used them as a metaphor for the House Un-American Activities Committee's "witch hunt" of purported communists. More importantly, it inspired his challenging of the idea of an "American Dream" built on materialism and conformity to conservative values. As Miller himself stated, "The American Dream is the largely unacknowledged screen in front of which all American writing plays itself out. Whoever is writing in the United States is using the American Dream as an ironical pole of his story. People elsewhere tend to accept, to a far greater degree anyway, that the conditions of life are hostile to man's pretensions." Individual moral responsibility in the face of oppression, injustice, and personal betrayals are paramount in Miller's plays. Failing, as Willy Loman does, to know his own true nature and embrace it is, in the final analysis, Miller's metaphor for a nation often faced with and often failing to stand behind its own ideals. An individual's moral convictions — and the willingness to live them — is the only accounting of a life Miller valued. His belief that theater could "change the world" as a moral agent never wavered. In his finest works, he articulated a nation's failings and its strengths. For Miller, a playwright "is nothing without his audience. He is the one of the audience who happens to know how to speak." Miller spoke for them through his characters. He made this point most vividly in his first important play, *All My Sons*, when the character Chris Keller says, "Once and for all you must know that there's a universe of people outside, and you're responsible for it."

DRAMATIC MOMENTS

from the Major Plays

These short excerpts are from the playwright's major plays. They give a taste of the work of the playwright. Each has a short introduction in brackets that helps the reader understand the context of the excerpt. The excerpts, which are in chronological order, illustrate the main themes mentioned in the In an Hour essay. Premiere date is provided.

from **The Man Who Had All the Luck** (1944)

from Act One

CHARACTERS

Pat
Shory
David
J.B.
Amos

[This play, subtitled "A Fable," was Arthur Miller's first Broadway production. In it, David Beeves, a twenty-two-year-old small-town businessman, mistrusts the good luck that comes his way while observing that his brother, Amos, has no luck at all. Early in the play, David's father, Pat, reflects on Amos's birth and becomes defensive about Amos's dreams of being a baseball player, which, despite his talents, have not produced the desired results.]

PAT: (*Rises to a self-induced froth of a climax.*) I always left David to concentrate for himself. But take Amos then. When I got back from the sea I came home and what do I find? An infant in his mother's arms. I felt his body and I saw it was strong. And I said to myself, this boy is not going to waste out his life being seventeen different kind of things and ending up nothing. He's going to play baseball. And by ginger he's been throwin' against the target down the cellar seven days a week for twelve solid years! That's concentration! That's faith! That's taking your life in your own hands and molding it to fit the thing you want. That's bound to have an effect . . . and don't you think they don't know it!

SHORY: Who knows it?

PAT: (*With a cry.*) I don't like everybody's attitude.

(Silence an instant. All staring at him.)

PAT: It's still winter! Can he play in winter?

SHORY: Who are you talking about?

DAVID: *(Going away — toward the right — bored and disgusted.)* Dad, he didn't say . . .

PAT: He doesn't have to say it. You people seem to think he's going to go through life pitching Sundays in the sand lots. *(To all.)* Pitching's his business; it's a regular business like . . . running a store, or being a mechanic or anything else. And it happens that in the winter there is nothing to do in his business but sit home and wait!

J.B.: Well, yeh, Pat, that's just what he ought to be doing.

PAT: Then why does everybody look at him as though . . . ?

(He raises his hand to his head, utterly confused and ashamed of his outburst. A long pause like this.)

DAVID: *(Unable to bear it, he goes to Pat.)* Sit down, Dad. Sit down. *(He gets a barrel under Pat, who sits, staring, exhausted.)*

PAT: I can't understand it. Every paper in the county calls him a phenomenon.

(As he speaks, David, feeling Pat's pain, goes right a few yards and stands looking away.)

PAT: Undefeated. He's ready for the big leagues. Been read for three years. Who can explain a thing like that? Why don't they send a scout?

DAVID: I been thinking about that, Dad. Maybe you ought to call the Detroit Tigers again.

AMOS: *(Peevishly. This has been in him a long time.)* He never called them in the first place.

PAT: Now, Amos . . .

DAVID: *(Reprimanding.)* Dad. . .

AMOS: He didn't. He didn't call them. *(To Pat.)* I want him to know!

DAVID: (*To Pat.*) But last summer you said . . .

PAT: I've picked up the phone a lot of time . . . but I . . . I wanted it to happen . . . naturally. It ought to happen naturally, Dave.

SHORY: You mean you don't want to hear them say no.

PAT: Well . . . yes, I admit that. (*To David.*) If I call now and demand an answer, maybe they'll have to say no. I don't want to put that word in their head in relation to Amos. It's a great psychological thing there. Once they refuse it's twice as hard to get them to accept.

DAVID: But, Dad, maybe . . . maybe they forgot to send a scout. Maybe they even thought they'd sent one and didn't, and when you call they'll thank you for reminding them. (*To all.*) I mean . . . can you *just wait for something to happen?*

from **The Man Who Had
All the Luck** (1944)
from Act Three

CHARACTERS

David
Gus
Hester

[David never gets an answer to questions about his good luck and the poor luck of his less fortunate friends and family. When a friend, Dan Dibble, also suffers a business reversal and, despite David's offers of help, decides he is too old to start over, David remains astonished about his own good luck and tortured by the sense that his own luck can evaporate at anytime.]

DAVID: I can't believe it. He's the best in the business.
GUS: Not any more.
HESTER: This wasn't something from the sky, dear. This was you only. You must see that now, don't you?

(The baby crying is heard from above.)

HESTER: I'd better go up, he's hungry. Come up? — Why don't you, Dave?
DAVID: (*Awkwardly.*) I will . . . right away.

(Hester exits. His face is rapt.)

DAVID: But they couldn't all have made their own luck! — J.B. with his drinking, Shory with his whores, Dad and Amos . . . and you losing your shop. (*Seizing on it.*) And I could never have fixed that Marmon if you hadn't walked in like some kind of angel! — that Marmon wasn't me!

GUS: You'd have towed it to Newton and fixed it there without me. (*Grasps David's hand.*) But is that really the question anyway? Of course bad things must happen. And you can't help it when God drops the other shoe. But whether you lay there or get up again — that's the part that's entirely up to you, that's for sure.

DAVID: You don't understand it either, do you?

GUS: No, but I live with it. All I know is you are a good man, but also you have luck. So you have to grin and bear it — you are lucky!

DAVID: For now.

GUS: Well, listen — "for now" is a very big piece of "forever."

HESTER: (*From above.*) Dave? You coming up?

GUS: Go on, kiss the little fellow.

DAVID: . . . I had the phone in my hand to call him. And I put it down. I had his whole ranch right here in my hand.

GUS: You mean you were a little bit like God . . . for him.

DAVID: Yes. Except I didn't know it.

GUS: (*A thumb pointing heavenward.*) Maybe he doesn't know either.

HESTER: (*From above.*) David? Are you there?

GUS: Goodnight, Dave.

DAVID: (*With a farewell wave to Gus, calls upstairs.*) Yes, I'm here! (*He goes to the stairs. A shock of thunder strikes. He quickly turns toward the windows, the old apprehension in his face.*) . . . (*To himself.*) For now. (*With a self-energized determination in his voice and body.*) Comin' up!

(*As he mounts the stairs a rumble of thunder sounds in the distance.*)

****

from **All My Sons** (1947)

from Act One

CHARACTERS

Keller
Ann

[During World War II, businessman Joe Keller shipped defective parts
for aircraft, causing the deaths of twenty-one American flyers. Initially
jailed, Joe puts the blame on an associate, Steve, and is released and
presumed innocent. Steve's daughter Ann, the fiancée of Joe's son
Larry, who was killed during the war, is now interested in Larry's
brother Chris. She comes to visit, and Joe, in an elaborate cover-up of
his own actions, attempts to justify Steve's.]

KELLER: The man was a fool, but don't make a murderer out of him.
You got no sense? Look what it does to her! (*To Ann.*) Listen, you
gotta appreciate what was doin' in that shop in the war. The both of
you! It was a madhouse. Every half hour the Major callin' for cylin-
der heads, they were whippin' us with the telephone. The trucks
were hauling them away hot, damn near. I mean just try to see it
human, see it human. All of a sudden a batch comes out with a crack.
That happens, that's the business. A fine, hairline crack. All right, so
— so he's a little man, your father, always scared of loud voices.
What'll the Major say? — Half a day's production shot. . . . What'll
I say? You know what I mean? Human. (*He pauses.*) So he takes out
his tools and he — covers over the cracks. All right — that's bad, it's
wrong, but that's what a little man does. If I could have gone in that
day I'd a told him — junk 'em, Steve, we can afford it. But alone he
was afraid. But I know he meant no harm. He believed they'd hold
up a hundred per cent. That's a mistake, but it ain't murder. You
mustn't feel that way about him. You understand me? It ain't right.

from **All My Sons** (1947)
from Act Two

CHARACTERS

Frank
Mother
Chris
George
Ann
Keller

[As Joe's deception begins to unravel, his wife, Kate, who suspects Joe's culpability, clings to the desperate belief that her son Larry, killed in the war, may be alive. George, the son of Joe's jailed business associate languishing in prison for Joe's acts, is endeavoring to prove his father's innocence to his sister, Ann, who is in love with Chris, Joe's surviving son.]

(Frank enters briskly from driveway, holding Larry's horoscope in his hand. He comes to Kate.)

FRANK: Kate! Kate!

MOTHER: Frank, did you see George?

FRANK: (*Extending his hand.*) Lydia told me, I'm glad to . . . you'll have to pardon me. (*Pulling Mother over.*) I've got something amazing for you, Kate, I finished Larry's horoscope.

MOTHER: You'd be interested in this, George. It's wonderful the way he can understand the —

CHRIS: (*Entering from house.*) George, the girl's on the phone —

MOTHER: (*Desperately.*) He finished Larry's horoscope!

CHRIS: Frank, can't you pick a better time than this?

FRANK: The greatest men who ever lived believed in the stars!

CHRIS: Stop filling her head with that junk!

FRANK: Is it junk to feel that there's a greater power than ourselves? I've studied the stars of his life! I won't argue with you, I'm telling you. Somewhere in this world your brother is alive!

MOTHER: (*Instantly to Chris.*) Why isn't it possible?

CHRIS: Because it's insane.

FRANK: Just a minute now. I'll tell you something and you can do as you please. Just let me say it. He was supposed to have died on November twenty-fifth. But November twenty-fifth was his favorable day.

CHRIS: Mother!

MOTHER: Listen to him!

FRANK: It was a day when everything good was shining on him, the kind of day he should've married on. You can laugh at a lot of it, I can understand you laughing. But the odds are a million to one that a man won't die on his favorable day. That's known, that's known, Chris.

MOTHER: Why isn't it possible, why isn't it possible, Chris!

GEORGE: (*To Ann.*) Don't you understand what she's saying? She just told you to go. What are you waiting for now?

CHRIS: Nobody can tell her to go.

(*A car horn is heard.*)

MOTHER: (*To Frank.*) Thank you, darling, for your trouble. Will you tell him to wait, Frank?

FRANK: (*As he goes.*) Sure thing.

MOTHER: (*Calling out.*) They'll be right out, driver!

CHRIS: She's not leaving, Mother.

GEORGE: You heard her say it, he's never been sick!

MOTHER: He misunderstood me, Chris! (*Chris looks at her, struck.*)

GEORGE: (*To Ann.*) He simply told your father to kill pilots, and covered himself in bed!

CHRIS: You'd better answer him, Annie. Answer him.

MOTHER: I packed your bag, darling.

CHRIS: What?

MOTHER: I packed your bag. All you've got to do is close it.

ANN: I'm not closing anything. He asked me here and I'm staying till he tells me to go. (*To George.*) Till Chris tells me!

CHRIS: That's all! Now get out of here, George!

MOTHER: (*To Chris.*) But if that's how he feels —

CHRIS: That's all, nothing more till Christ comes, about the case or Larry as long as I'm here! (*To George.*) Now get out of here, George!

GEORGE: (*To Ann.*) You tell me. I want to hear you tell me.

ANN: Go, George!

(*They disappear up the driveway, Ann saying, "Don't take it that way, Georgie! Please don't take it that way."*)

CHRIS: (*Turning to his mother.*) What do you mean, you packed her bag? How dare you pack her bag?

MOTHER: Chris —

CHRIS: How dare you pack her bag?

MOTHER: She doesn't belong here.

CHRIS: Then I don't belong here.

MOTHER: She's Larry's girl.

CHRIS: And I'm his brother and he's dead, and I'm marrying his girl.

MOTHER: Never, never in this world!

KELLER: You lost your mind?

MOTHER: You have nothing to say!

KELLER: (*Cruelly.*) I got plenty to say. Three and a half years you been talking like a maniac —

(*Mother smashes him across the face.*)

MOTHER: Nothing. You have nothing to say. Now I say. He's coming back, and everybody has got to wait.

CHRIS: Mother, Mother —

MOTHER: Wait, wait —

CHRIS: How long? How long?

MOTHER: (*Rolling out of her.*) Till he comes; forever and ever till he comes!

CHRIS: (*As an ultimatum.*) Mother, I'm going ahead with it.

MOTHER: Chris, I've never said no to you in my life, now I say no!

CHRIS: You'll never let him go till I do it.

MOTHER: I'll never let him go and you'll never let him go!

CHRIS: I've let him go. I've let him go a long —

MOTHER: (*With no less force, but turning from him.*) Then let your father go.

(*Pause. Chris stands transfixed.*)

KELLER: She's out of her mind.

MOTHER: Altogether! (*To Chris, but not facing them.*) Your brother's alive, darling, because if he's dead, your father killed him. Do you understand me now? As long as you live, that boy is alive. God does not let a son be killed by his father. Now you see, don't you? Now you see. (*Beyond control, she hurries up and into the house.*)

KELLER: (*Chris has not moved. He speaks insinuatingly, questioningly.*) She's out of her mind.

CHRIS: (*In a broken whisper.*) Then . . . you did it?

KELLER: (*With the beginning of a plea in his voice.*) He never flew a P 40 —

CHRIS: (*Struck; deadly.*) But the others.

KELLER: (*Insistently*) She's out of her mind. (*He takes a step toward Chris, pleadingly.*)

CHRIS: (*Unyielding.*) Dad . . . you did it?

(*Both hold their voices down.*)

KELLER: (*Afraid of him, his deadly insistence.*) What's the matter with you? What the hell is the matter with you?

CHRIS: Dad . . . Dad, you killed twenty-one men!

KELLER: What, killed?

CHRIS: You killed them, you murdered them.

KELLER: (*As though throwing his whole nature open before Chris.*) How could I kill anybody?

CHRIS: Dad! Dad!

KELLER: (*Trying to hush him.*) I didn't kill anybody!

CHRIS: Then explain it to me. What did you do? Explain it to me or I'll tear you to pieces!

KELLER: (*Horrified at his overwhelming fury.*) Don't, Chris, don't —

CHRIS: I want to know what you did, now what did you do? You had a hundred and twenty cracked engine-heads, now what did you do?

KELLER: If you're going to hang me then I —

CHRIS: I'm listening. God Almighty, I'm listening!

KELLER: (*Their movements now are those of subtle pursuit and escape. Keller keeps a step out of Chris's range as he talks.*) You're a boy, what could I do! I'm in business, a man of business; a hundred and twenty cracked, you're out of business; you got a process, the process don't work you're out of business; you don't know how to operate, your stuff no good; they close you up, they tear up your contracts, what the hell's it to them? You lay forty years into a business and they knock you out in five minutes, what could I do, let them take forty years, let them take my life away? (*His voice cracking.*) I never thought they'd install them. I swear to God. I thought they'd stop 'em before anybody took off.

CHRIS: Then why'd you ship them out?

KELLER: By the time they could spot them I thought I'd have the process going again, and I could show them they needed me and they'd let it go by. But weeks passed and I got no kick-back, so I was going to tell them.

CHRIS: Then why didn't you tell them?

KELLER: It was too late. The paper, it was all over the front pages, twenty-one went down, it was too late. They came with handcuffs into the shop, what could I do? (*He sits on bench.*) Chris . . . Chris, I did it for you, it was a chance and I took it for you. I'm sixty-one years old. You don't get another chance, do ya?

CHRIS: You even knew they wouldn't hold up in the air.

KELLER: I didn't say that.

CHRIS: But you were going to warn them not to use them —

KELLER: But that don't mean —

CHRIS: It means you knew they'd crash.

KELLER: It don't mean that.

CHRIS: Then you *thought* they'd crash.

KELLER: I was afraid maybe —

CHRIS: You were afraid maybe! God in heaven, what kind of a man are you? Kids were hanging in the air by those heads. You knew that!

KELLER: For you, a business for you!

CHRIS: (*With burning fury.*) For me! Where do you live, where have you come from? For me! — I was dying every day and you were killing my boys and you did it for me? What the hell do you think I was thinking of, the Goddam business? Is that as far as your mind can see, the business? What is that, the world — the business? What the hell do you mean, you did it for me? Don't you have a country? Don't you live in the world? What the hell are you? You're not even an animal, no animal kills his own, what are you? What must I do to you? I ought to tear the tongue out of your mouth, what must I do? (*With his fist he pounds down upon his father's shoulder. He stumbles away, covering his face as he weeps.*) What must I do, Jesus God, what must I do?

KELLER: Chris . . . My Chris . . .

CHARACTERS

Chris
Mother
Ann

[As *All My Sons* draws to a close, Chris, now aware of the fact that his father, Joe, is the responsible party in the manufacture of faulty parts leading to the deaths of twenty-one flyers, grapples with how to deal with the situation and his relationship with Ann, the daughter of the man framed for Joe's actions.]

CHRIS: Mother . . . I'm going away. There are a couple of firms in Cleveland, I think I can get a place. I mean, I'm going away for good. (*To Ann alone.*) I know what you're thinking, Annie. It's true. I'm yellow. I was made yellow in this house because I suspected my father and I did nothing about it, but if I knew that night when I came home what I know now, he'd be in the district attorney's office by this time, and I'd have brought him there. Now if I look at him, all I'm able to do is cry.

****

from **Death of a Salesman** (1949)
from Act One

CHARACTERS

Linda
Willy
Charley
Happy
Biff

[Aging traveling salesman Willy Loman, haunted by memories of his past (accompanied by the sounds of a flute) and the failure of his career, returns home from a sales trip unexpectedly.]

LINDA: (*Hearing Willy outside the bedroom, calls with some trepidation.*) Willy!

WILLY: It's all right. I came back.

LINDA: Why? What happened? (*Slight pause.*) Did something happen, Willy?

WILLY: No, nothing happened.

LINDA: You didn't smash the car, did you?

WILLY: (*With casual irritation.*) I said nothing happened. Didn't you hear me?

LINDA: Don't you feel well?

WILLY: I'm tired to death. (*The flute has faded away. He sits on the bed beside her, a little numb.*) I couldn't make it. I just couldn't make it, Linda.

LINDA: (*Very carefully, delicately.*) Where were you all day? You look terrible.

WILLY: I got as far as a little above Yonkers. I stopped for a cup of coffee. Maybe it was the coffee.

LINDA: What?

WILLY: (*After a pause.*) I suddenly couldn't drive any more. The car kept going off the shoulder, y'know?

LINDA: (*Helpfully.*) Oh. Maybe it was the steering again. I don't think Angelo knows the Studebaker.

WILLY: No, it's me, it's me. Suddenly I realize I'm goin' sixty miles an hour and I don't remember the last five minutes. I'm — I can't seem to — keep my mind to it.

[As the scene continues, Happy and Biff, the grown sons of Willy and Linda, awaken and share their concern about the obviously distressed Willy's state. Memories of happier times are tinged by Biff's sense of entitlement, aggressively encouraged by Willy. Other memories, including Willy's extramarital affair with The Woman, an otherwise unnamed character, crowd in. Willy's mumbling becomes louder to the point that his next door neighbor and only friend, Charley, comes to the Loman's kitchen. Charley is a supportive friend, but his kindness is difficult for Willy, who imagines himself as superior, to accept.]

CHARLEY: Everything all right?

HAPPY: Yeah, Charley, everything's . . .

WILLY: What's the matter?

CHARLEY: I heard some noise. I thought something happened. Can't we do something about these walls? You sneeze in here, and in my house hats blow off.

HAPPY: Let's go to bed, Dad. Come on.

(*Charley signals to Happy to go.*)

WILLY: You go ahead, I'm not tired at the moment.

HAPPY: (*To Willy.*) Take it easy, huh? (*He exits.*)

WILLY: What're you doin' up?

CHARLEY: (*Sitting down at the kitchen table opposite Willy.*) Couldn't sleep good. I had a heartburn.

WILLY: Well, you don't know how to eat.

CHARLEY: I eat with my mouth.

WILLY: No, you're ignorant. You gotta know about vitamins and things like that.

CHARLEY: Come on, let's shoot. Tire you out a little.

WILLY: (*Hesitantly.*) All right. You got cards?

CHARLEY: (*Taking a deck from his pocket.*) Yeah, I got them. Someplace. What is it with those vitamins?

WILLY: (*Dealing.*) They build up your bones. Chemistry.

CHARLEY: Yeah, but there's no bones in a heartburn.

WILLY: What are you talkin' about? Do you know the first thing about it?

CHARLEY: Don't get insulted.

WILLY: Don't talk about something you don't know anything about.

(They are playing. Pause.)

CHARLEY: What're you doin' home?

WILLY: A little trouble with the car.

CHARLEY: Oh. (*Pause.*) I'd like to take a trip to California.

WILLY: Don't say.

CHARLEY: You want a job?

WILLY: I got a job, I told you that. (*After a slight pause.*) What the hell are you offering me a job for?

CHARLEY: Don't get insulted.

WILLY: Don't insult me.

CHARLEY: I don't see no sense in it. You don't have to go on this way.

WILLY: I got a good job. (*Slight pause.*) What do you keep comin' in here for?

CHARLEY: You want me to go?

WILLY: (*After a pause, withering.*) I can't understand it. He's going back to Texas again. What the hell is that?

CHARLEY: Let him go.

WILLY: I got nothin' to give him, Charley, I'm clean, I'm clean.

CHARLEY: He won't starve. None a them starve. Forget about him.

WILLY: Then what have I got to remember?

(As Willy slips further into the past, Biff expresses his concerns to Linda, who confronts him about both his lack of concern and his future.)

LINDA: When you write you're coming home, he's all smiles, and talks about the future, and — he's just wonderful. And then the closer you seem to come, the more shaky he gets, and then, by the time you get here, he's arguing, and he seems angry at you. I think it's just that maybe he can't bring himself to — to open up to you. Why are you so hateful to each other? Why is that?

BIFF: *(Evasively.)* I'm not hateful, Mom.

LINDA: But you no sooner come in the door than you're fighting!

BIFF: I don't know why. I mean to change. I'm tryin', Mom, you understand?

LINDA: Are you home to stay now?

BIFF: I don't know. I want to look around, see what's doin'.

LINDA: Biff, you can't look around all your life, can you?

BIFF: I just can't take hold, Mom. I can't take hold of some kind of life.

[As the first act of *Death of a Salesman* ends, Willy tenuously holds on to both his sanity and his hopes for Biff's future.]

from **Death of a Salesman** (1949)

from Act Two

CHARACTERS

Willy
Biff
The Woman

[A new day brings forth a somewhat revived Willy Loman, but things rapidly spiral downward when he is fired from his job by Howard, the son of the man who first employed him. Willy has nowhere to turn, but finds himself at Charley's office, where Bernard, Charley's son, who is about to argue his first case before the Supreme Court, is waiting. Bernard's success adds to Willy's distress about Biff's inability to find a career path or satisfying existence. Bernard cannot help Willy, who struggles to comprehend why Biff has not achieved Bernard's level of success. Willy goes to a restaurant to meet Biff and Happy and sinks further into the past, finally arriving at the critical moment when, while he was on the road in a Boston hotel room with The Woman, his relationship with Biff came to a head. Biff unexpectedly turns up seeking Willy's help after he learns he has flunked a math class that will prevent him from graduating high school. When Biff arrives, Willy is forced to hide The Woman in the bathroom.]

BIFF: Oh, Dad, good work! I'm sure he'll change it for you!

WILLY: Go downstairs and tell the clerk I'm checkin' out. Go right down.

BIFF: Yes, sir! See, the reason he hate me, Pop — one day he was late for class so I got up at the blackboard and imitated him. I crossed my eyes and talked with a lithp.

WILLY: (*Laughing.*) You did? The kids like it?

BIFF: They nearly died laughing!

WILLY: Yeah? What'd you do?
BIFF: The thquare root of thixthy twee is . . .

(Willy bursts out laughing; Biff joins him.)

BIFF: And in the middle of it he walked in!

(Willy laughs and The Woman joins in offstage.)

WILLY: *(Without hesitation.)* Hurry downstairs and —
BIFF: Somebody in there?
WILLY: No, that was next door.

(The Woman laughs offstage.)

BIFF: Somebody got in your bathroom!
WILLY: No, it's the next room, there's a party —

(The Woman enters, laughing. She lisps this: Can I come in? There's
something in the bathtub, Willy, and it's moving!*)*

WILLY: Ah — you better go back to your room. They must be finished
    painting by now. They're painting her room so I let her take a
    shower here. Go back, go back . . . *(He pushes her.)*
THE WOMAN: *(Resisting.)* But I've got to get dressed, Willy, I can't —
WILLY: Get out of here! Go back, go back . . . *(Suddenly striving for the
    ordinary.)* This is Miss Francis, Biff, she's a buyer. They're painting
    her room. Go back, Miss Francis, go back . . .
THE WOMAN: But my clothes, I can't go out naked in the hall!
WILLY: *(Pushing her offstage.)* Get outa here! Go back, go back!

(Biff slowly sits down on his suitcase as the argument continues offstage.)

THE WOMAN: Where's my stockings! You promised me stockings,
    Willy!
WILLY: I have no stockings here!

THE WOMAN: You had two boxes of size nine sheers for me, and I want them!

WILLY: Here, for God's sake, will you get outa here!

THE WOMAN: (*Enters holding a box of stockings.*) I just hope there's nobody in the hall. That's all I hope. (*To Biff.*) Are you football or baseball?

BIFF: Football.

THE WOMAN: (*Angry, humiliated.*) That's me too. G'night. (*She snatches her clothes from Willy, and walks out.*)

WILLY: (*After a pause.*) Well, better get going. I want to get to the school first thing in the morning. Get my suits out of the closet. I'll get my valise.

(*Biff doesn't move.*)

WILLY: What's the matter?

(*Biff remains motionless, tears falling.*)

WILLY: She's a buyer. Buys for J. H. Simmons. She lives down the hall — they're painting. You don't imagine — (*He breaks off. After a pause.*) Now listen, pal, she just a buyer. She sees merchandise in her room and they have to keep it looking just so . . . (*Pause. Assuming command.*) All right, get my suits.

(*Biff doesn't move.*)

WILLY: Now stop crying and do as I say. I gave you an order. Biff, I gave you an order! Is that what you do when I give you an order? How dare you cry! (*Putting his arm around Biff.*) Now look, Biff, when you grow up you'll understand about these things. You mustn't — you mustn't overemphasize a thing like this. I'll see Birnbaum first thing in the morning.

BIFF: Never mind.

WILLY: (*Getting down beside Biff.*) Never mind! He's going to give you those points. I'll see to it.

BIFF: He wouldn't listen to you.

WILLY: He certainly will listen to me. You need those points for the U. of Virginia.

BIFF: I'm not going there.

WILLY: Heh? If I can't get him to change that mark you'll make it up in summer school. You've got all summer to —

BIFF: (*His weeping breaking from him.*) Dad . . .

WILLY: (*Infected by it.*) Oh, my boy . . .

BIFF: Dad . . .

WILLY: She's nothing to me, Biff. I was lonely, I was terribly lonely.

BIFF: You — you gave her Mama's stockings! His tears break through and he rises to go.

WILLY: (*Grabbing for Biff.*) I gave you an order!

BIFF: Don't touch me, you — liar!

WILLY: Apologize for that!

BIFF: You fake! You phony little fake! You fake! (*Overcome, he turns quickly and weeping fully goes out with his suitcase. Willy is left on the floor on his knees.*)

WILLY: I gave you an order! Biff, come back here or I'll beat you! Come back here! I'll whip you!

[Abandoned in the restaurant by his sons, Willy staggers home, encountering the memory of his brother, Ben, in an imagined conversation in which he reasons that his suicide will bring Biff the benefit of his life insurance, $20,000, which, in Willy's distressed mind, will provide Biff with one last opportunity for success. Linda attempts to bring some peace to the boys and their father, as all go off to bed except Willy, who tells Linda he will join her in two minutes. Instead, he again converses with Ben, deciding to commit suicide. The play ends at Willy's graveside.]

from **Death of a Salesman** (1949)

from Requiem

CHARACTERS

Charley
Biff
Happy
Linda
Bernard

[Biff, Happy, and Charley stand by Linda following Willy's burial. There are no crowds because Willy is not known — and while Linda mourns, the sons argue over Willy's life. Finally, Charley offers an ultimate statement on Willy Loman.]

CHARLEY: (*Stopping Happy's movement and reply. To Biff.*) Nobody dast blame this man. You don't understand: Willy was a salesman. And for a salesman, there is no rock bottom to the life. He don't put a bolt to a nut, he don't tell you the law or give you medicine. He's a man way out there in the blue, riding on a smile and a shoeshine. And when they start not smiling back — that's an earthquake. And then you get yourself a couple of spots on your hat, and you're finished. Nobody dast blame this man. A salesman is got to dream, boy. It comes with the territory.

BIFF: Charley, the man didn't know who he was.

HAPPY: (*Infuriated.*) Don't say that!

BIFF: Why don't you come with me, Happy?

HAPPY: I'm not licked that easily. I'm staying right in this city, and I'm gonna beat this racket! (*He looks at Biff, his chin set.*) The Loman Brothers!

BIFF: I know who I am, kid.

HAPPY: All right, boy. I'm gonna show you and everybody else that

Willy Loman did not die in vain. He had a good dream. It's the only dream you can have — to come out number-one man. He fought it out here, and this is where I'm gonna win it for him.

BIFF: (*With a hopeless glance at Happy, bends toward his mo*ther.) Let's go, Mom.

LINDA: I'll be with you in a minute. Go on, Charley.

(*He hesitates.*)

LINDA: I want to, just for a minute. I never had a chance to say good-bye.

(*Charley moves away followed by Happy. Biff remains a slight distance up and left of Linda. She sits there, summoning herself. The flute begins, not far away, playing behind her speech.*)

LINDA: Forgive me, dear. I can't cry. I don't know what it is, but I can't cry. I don't understand it. Why did you ever do that? Help me, Willy, I can't cry. It seems to me that you're just on another trip. I keep expecting you. Willy, dear, I can't cry. Why did you do it? I search and search and I search, and I can't understand it, Willy. I made the last payment on the house today. Today, dear. And there'll be nobody home. (*A sob rises in her throat.*) We're free and clear. (*Sobbing more fully, released.*) We're free.

(*Biff comes slowly toward her.*)

LINDA: We're free . . . We're free . . .

(*Biff lifts her to her feet and moves out right with her in his arms. Linda sobs quietly. Bernard and Charley come together and follow them, followed by Happy. Only the music of the flute is left on the darkening stage as over the house the hard towers of the apartment buildings rise into sharp focus.*)

CURTAIN

****

from **The Crucible** (1953)
from Act One

CHARACTERS

> Abigail
> Parris
> Proctor

[Set in 1692 in Salem, Massachusetts, during a tragic period of local hysteria, *The Crucible* begins shortly after an incident in which some young girls, accused of blasphemy for dancing in the nearby woods after dark, are facing harsh consequences. They manage, through the wiles of Abigail Williams, their manipulative ringleader, to turn the tables by accusing local citizens of witchcraft. As Betty Parris, daughter of Reverend Parris and one of the girls caught dancing, lies in a trance-like state induced by her fear of her father's retribution, Abigail, Parris's niece, is brought before him for questioning.]

PARRIS: (*Studies her, then nods, half convinced.*) Abigail, I have fought here three long years to bend these stiff-necked people to me, and now, just now when some good respect is rising for me in the parish, you compromise my very character. I have given you a home, child, I have put clothes upon your back — now give me an upright answer. Your name in the town — it is entirely white, is it not?

ABIGAIL: (*With an edge of resentment.*) Why, I am sure it is, sir. There be no blush about my name.

PARRIS: (*To the point.*) Abigail, is there any other cause than you have told me, for your being discharged from Goody Proctor's service? I have heard it said, and I tell you as I heard it, that she comes so rarely to the church this year for she will not sit so close to something soiled. What signified that remark?

ABIGAIL: She hates me, uncle, she must, for I would not be her slave. It's a bitter woman, a lying, cold, sniveling woman, and I will not work for such a woman!

PARRIS: She may be. And yet it has troubled me that you are now seven month out of their house, and in all this time no other family has ever called for your service.

ABIGAIL: They want slaves, not such as I. Let them send to Barbados for that. I will not black my face for any of them! (*With ill-concealed resentment at him.*) Do you begrudge my bed, uncle?

PARRIS: No — no.

ABIGAIL: (*In a temper.*) My name is good in the village! I will not have it said my name is soiled! Goody Proctor is a gossiping liar!

[In fact, Abigail's dismissal from service at the Proctor home resulted from Elizabeth Proctor's knowledge that her husband, John, committed a sexual indiscretion with Abigail. John has asked forgiveness and demonstrated his remorse and Elizabeth has forgiven him, but kept him at arm's length. As Abigail whips up hysteria over witchcraft in Salem, she confronts John, who has assiduously avoided her since Elizabeth dismissed her from their home.]

ABIGAIL: Give me a word, John. A soft word. (*Her concentrated desire destroys his smile.*)

PROCTOR: No, no, Abby. That's done with.

ABIGAIL: (*Tauntingly.*) You come five mile to see a silly girl fly?

PROCTOR: (*Setting her firmly out of his path.*) I come to see what mischief your uncle's brewin' now. (*With final emphasis.*) Put it out of mind, Abby.

ABIGAIL: (*Grasping his hand before he can release her.*) John — I am waitin' for you every night.

PROCTOR: Abby, I never give you hope to wait for me.

ABIGAIL: (*Now beginning to anger — she can't believe it.*) I have something better than hope, I think!

PROCTOR: Abby, you'll put it out of your mind. I'll not be comin' for you more.

ABIGAIL: You're surely sportin' with me.

PROCTOR: You know me better.

ABIGAIL: I know how you clutched my back behind your house and sweated like a stallion whenever I come near! Or did I dream that? It's she put me out, you cannot pretend it were you. I saw your face when she put me out, and you loved me then and you do now!

PROCTOR: Abby, that's a wild thing to say —

ABIGAIL: A wild thing may say wild things. But not so wild, I think. I have seen you since she put me out; I have seen you nights.

PROCTOR: I have hardly stepped off my farm this sevenmonth.

ABIGAIL: I have a sense for heat, John, and yours has drawn me to my window, and I have seen you looking up, burning in your loneliness. Do you tell me you've never looked up at my window?

PROCTOR: I may have looked up.

ABIGAIL: (*Now softening.*) And you must. You are no wintry man. I know you, John. I *know* you. (*She is weeping.*) I cannot sleep for dreamin'; I cannot dream but I wake and walk about the house as though I'd find you comin' through some door. (*She clutches him desperately.*)

PROCTOR: (*Gently pressing her from him, with great sympathy but firmly.*) Child —

ABIGAIL: (*With a flash of anger.*) How do you call me child!

PROCTOR: Abby, I may think of you softly from time to time. But I will cut off my hand before I'll ever reach for you again. Wipe it out of mind. We never touched, Abby.

from **The Crucible** (1953)
from Act Two

CHARACTERS

Elizabeth
Proctor

[Various state officials and religious leaders come to Salem to seek the truth about the witchcraft accusations as Abigail, infuriated by Proctor's rejection, realizes the power with which her accusations endow her. As time goes by, matters escalate in Salem as local citizens accused of witchcraft are brought before the authorities. The accused are shown leniency if they identify others allegedly practicing witchcraft. Tensions increase in the Proctor household as Elizabeth and John discuss the situation, revealing the troubles in their marriage.]

PROCTOR: Woman. (*She turns to him.*) I'll not have your suspicion any more.

ELIZABETH: (*A little loftily.*) I have no —

PROCTOR: I'll not have it!

ELIZABETH: Then let you not earn it.

PROCTOR: (*With a violent undertone.*) You doubt me yet?

ELIZABETH: (*With a smile, to keep her dignity.*) John, if it were not Abigail that you must go to hurt, would you falter now? I think not.

PROCTOR: Now look you —

ELIZABETH: I see what I see, John.

PROCTOR: (*With solemn warning.*) You will not judge me more, Elizabeth. I have good reason to think before I charge fraud on Abigail, and I will think on it. Let you look to your own improvement before you go to judge your husband any more. I have forgot Abigail, and —

ELIZABETH: And I.

PROCTOR: Spare me! You forget nothin' and forgive nothin'. Learn charity, woman. I have gone tiptoe in this house all seven months since she is gone. I have not moved from there to there without I think to please you, and still an everlasting funeral marches round your heart. I cannot speak but I am doubted, every moment judged for lies, as though I come into a court when I come into this house!

ELIZABETH: John, you are not open with me. You saw her with a crowd, you said. Now you —

PROCTOR: I'll plead my honesty no more, Elizabeth.

ELIZABETH: (*Now she would justify herself.*) John, I am only —

PROCTOR: No more! I should have roared you down when first you told me your suspicion. But I wilted, and like a Christian, I confessed. Confessed! Some dream I had must have mistaken you for God that day. But you're not, you're not, and let you remember it! Let you look sometimes for the goodness in me, and judge me not.

ELIZABETH: I do not judge you. The magistrate sits in your heart that judges you. I never thought you but a good man, John — (*With a smile.*) only somewhat bewildered.

PROCTOR: (*Laughing bitterly.*) Oh, Elizabeth, your justice would freeze beer!

from **The Crucible** (1953)
from Act Four

CHARACTERS

> Danforth
> Proctor
> Parris
> Hale
> Elizabeth
> Rebecca

[The situation deteriorates, and both Proctors stand accused. Proctor is persuaded to save his own life by signing a false confession and accusing others, but in the final analysis he cannot speak his lie. He explains himself while under interrogation by the authorities.]

DANFORTH: Mr. Proctor, I must have good and legal proof that you —

PROCTOR: You are the high court, your word is good enough! Tell them I confessed myself; say Proctor broke his knees and wept like a woman; say what you will, but my name cannot —

DANFORTH: (*With suspicion.*) It is the same, is it not? If I report it or you sign to it?

PROCTOR: (*He knows it is insane.*) No, it is not the same! What others say and what I sign to is not the same!

DANFORTH: Why? Do you mean to deny this confession when you are free?

PROCTOR: I mean to deny nothing!

DANFORTH: Then explain to me, Mr. Proctor, why you will not let —

PROCTOR: (*With a cry of his whole soul.*) Because it is my name! Because I cannot have another in my life! Because I lie and sign myself to lies! Because I am not worth the dust on the feel of them that hang!

How may I live without my name? I have given you my soul; leave me my name!

DANFORTH: (*Pointing at the confession in Proctor's hand.*) Is that document a lie? If it is a lie I will not accept it! What say you? I will not deal in lies, Mister!

(*Proctor is motionless.*)

DANFORTH: You will give me your honest confession in my hand, or I cannot keep you from the rope.

(*Proctor does not reply.*)

DANFORTH: What way do you go, Mister?

(*His breast heaving, his eye staring, Proctor tears the paper and crumples it, and he is weeping in fury, but erect.*)

DANFORTH: Marshal!

PARRIS: (*Hysterically, as though the tearing paper were his life.*) Proctor, Proctor!

HALE: Man, you will hang! You cannot!

PROCTOR: (*His eyes full of tears.*) I can. And there's your first marvel, that I can. You have made your magic now, for now I do think I see some shred of goodness in John Proctor. Not enough to weave a banner with, but white enough to keep it from such dogs.

(*Elizabeth, in a burst of terror, rushes to him and weeps against his hand.*)

PROCTOR: Give them no tear! Tears pleasure them! Show honor now, show a stony heart and sink them with it! (*He has lifted her, and kisses her now with great passion.*)

REBECCA: Let you fear nothing! Another judgment waits us all!

DANFORTH: Hang them high over the town! Who weeps for these, weeps for corruption!

****

from **A View from the Bridge** (1955)

from Act One

CHARACTERS

Eddie

Alfieri

[Eddie Carbone, an Italian longshoreman, has, along with his wife, Beatrice, raised his niece, Catherine, from childhood. Now a grown woman, she has fallen in love with a young Italian man, Rodolpho, an illegal immigrant. When Eddie learns of Catherine's love for Rodolpho, his reaction is extreme, and it appears his feelings for Catherine border on the inappropriate. In order to stop Rodolpho from further contact with Catherine, Eddie turns to a lawyer, Alfieri.]

EDDIE: Mr. Alfieri, I can't believe what you tell me. I mean there must be some kinda law which —

ALFIERI: Eddie, I want you to listen to me. (*Pause.*) You know, sometimes God mixes up the people. We all love somebody, the wife, the kids — every man's got somebody he loves, heh? But sometimes . . . there's too much. You know? There's too much, and it goes where it mustn't. A man works hard, he brings up a child, sometimes it's niece, sometimes even a daughter, and he never realizes it, but through the years — there is too much love for the daughter, there is too much love for the niece. Do you understand what I'm saying to you?

EDDIE: (*Sardonically.*) What do you mean, I shouldn't look out for her good?

ALFIERI: Yes, but these things have to end, Eddie, that's all. The child has to grow up and go away, and the man has to learn to forget. Because after all, Eddie — what other way can it end? (*Pause.*) Let her go. That's my advice. You did your job, now it's her life; wish her luck, and let her go. (*Pause.*) Will you do that? Because there's no law, Eddie; make up your mind to it; the law is not interested in this.

EDDIE: You mean to tell me, even if he's a punk? If he's —

ALFIERI: There's nothing you can do.

(*Eddie stands.*)

EDDIE: Well, all right, thanks. Thanks very much.

ALFIERI: What are you going to do?

EDDIE: (*With a helpless but ironic gesture.*) What can I do? I'm a patsy, what can a patsy do? I worked like a dog twenty years so a punk could have her, so that's what I done. I mean, in the worst times, in the worst, when there wasn't a ship comin' in the harbor, I didn't stand around lookin' for relief — I hustled. When there was empty piers in Brooklyn I went to Hoboken, Staten Island, the West Side, Jersey, all over — because I made a promise. I took out of my own mouth to give to her. I took out of my wife's mouth. I walked hungry plenty of days in this city! (*It begins to break through.*) And I now I gotta sit in my own house and look at a son-of-a-bitch punk like that — which he came out of nowhere! I give him my house to sleep! I take the blankets off my bed for him, and he takes and puts his filthy hands on her like a goddam thief!

ALFIERI: (*Rising.*) But, Eddie, she's a woman now.

EDDIE: He's stealing from me!

ALFIERI: She wants to get married, Eddie. She can't marry you, can she?

EDDIE: (*Furiously.*) What're you talkin' about, marry me! I don't know what the hell you're talkin' about!

(*Pause.*)

ALFIERI: I gave you my advice, Eddie. That's it.

(*Eddie gathers himself. A pause.*)

EDDIE: Well, thanks. Thanks very much. It just — it's breakin' my heart, y'know. I —

ALFIERI: I understand. Put it out of your mind. Can you do that?

EDDIE: I'm — *He feels the threat of sobs, and with a helpless wave*). I'll see you around. (*He goes out up the right ramp.*)

ALFIERI: (*Sits on desk.*) There are times when you want to spread an alarm, but nothing has happened. I knew, I knew then and there — I could have finished the whole story that afternoon. It wasn't as though there was a mystery to unravel. I could see every step coming, step after step, like a dark figure walking down a hall toward a certain door. I knew where he was heading for, I knew where he was going to end. And I sat here many afternoons asking myself why, being an intelligent man, I was so powerless to stop it. I even went to a certain old lady in the neighborhood, a very wise ole woman, and I told her, and she only nodded, and said, "Pray for him . . ." And so I — waited there.

[As Alfieri feared, Eddie acted on his heartbroken confusion. He informed the immigration authorities of the presence of Rodolpho and his friend Marco. When he learns of Eddie's betrayal, Marco and Eddie fight. A struggle for a knife ends in Eddie's mortal wounding. He dies in the arms of his wife, Beatrice, while Catherine cries, "Eddie I never meant to do nothing bad to you." Alfieri, the observer of the play's action, reflects as the curtain falls.]

ALFIERI: Most of the time now we settle for half and I like it better. But the truth is holy, and even as I know how wrong he was, and his death useless, I tremble, for I confess that something perversely pure calls to me from his memory — not purely good, but himself purely, for he allowed himself to be wholly known and for that I think I will love him more than all my sensible clients. And yet, it is better to settle for half, it must be! And so I mourn him — I admit it — with a certain . . . alarm.

CURTAIN

****

THE READING ROOM

YOUNG ACTORS AND THEIR TEACHERS

Abbotson, Susan C. W. *Critical Companion to Arthur Miller: A Literary Reference to His Life and Work.* New York: Facts on File, 2007.

Bigsby, Christopher, ed. *The Portable Arthur Miller.* Revised Edition. New York: Penguin, 1995.

Bigsby, Christopher. *Remembering Arthur Miller.* London: A&C Black, 2005.

Bloom, Harold. *Arthur Miller.* Bloom's Modern Critical Views. New York: Chelsea House, 2007.

Bloom, Harold, ed. *Arthur Miller's All My Sons.* Bloom's Modern Critical Interpretations. New York: Chelsea House Publishers, 1987.

Bloom, Harold, ed. *Modern Literary Characters: Willy Loman.* New York: Chelsea House Publishers, 1990.

Bloom, Harold, and Albert A. Borg, eds. *Arthur Miller's Death of a Salesman.* Bloom's Guides. New York: Chelsea House Publishers, 2003.

Bloom, Harold, ed. *Arthur Miller's The Crucible.* Bloom's Modern Critical Interpretations. New York: Chelsea House Publishers, 2008.

Bly, William. *Arthur Miller's The Crucible.* Hauppauge, N.Y.: Barron's Educational Series, 1984.

Brater, Enoch. *Arthur Miller: A Playwright's Life and Works.* London: Thames & Hudson, 2005.

Griffin, Alice. *Understanding Arthur Miller.* Columbia: University of South Carolina Press, 1996.

Gussow, Mel, ed. *Conversations with Miller.* New York: Applause Books, 2002.

Harris, Andrew B. *Broadway Theatre.* London: Routledge, 1994.

This extensive bibliography lists books about the playwright according to whom the books might be of interest. If you would like to research further something that interests you in the text, lists of references, sources cited, and editions used in this book are found in this section.

Krasner, David. *A Companion to Twentieth-Century American Drama*. Blackwell, 2004.

Kushner, Tony, ed. *Arthur Miller: Collected Plays 1944–1961*. New York: Library of America, 2006.

Last, Brian W. *Arthur Miller, Death of a Salesman: Notes*. London: Longman, 1980.

Miller, Arthur. "The Man Who Had All the Luck," *Cross-section: A Collection of New American Writing*, ed. Edwin Seaver, New York: Fischer, 1944.

_____. "A Boy Grew in Brooklyn," *Holiday*, March 1955.

_____. *Timebends: A Life*. New York: Grove Press, 1987.

_____. "Introduction," *Chapters from My Autobiography* by Mark Twain. New York: Oxford University Press, 1996.

_____. *The Misfits: Story of a Shoot*, with Serge Toubiana, New York: Phaidon Press Inc., 2000.

_____. "Afterword," *Calder in Connecticut* by Alexander S. Rower and Eric Zafran. New York: Rizzoli International Publications, 2000.

Moss, Leonard. *Arthur Miller*. Boston: Twayne, 1980.

Murphy, Brenda. *Miller: Death of a Salesman*. New York: Cambridge University Press, 1995.

Murray, Edward. *Arthur Miller, Dramatist*. New York: Frederick Ungar Publishing, 1967.

Nelson, Benjamin. *Arthur Miller: Portrait of a Playwright*. New York: David McKay Company, 1970.

Partridge, C. J. *Death of a Salesman*, Oxford: Blackwell, 1969.

_____. *The Crucible*. Oxford: Blackwell, 1971.

Roudané, Matthew C. *American Drama Since 1960: A Critical History*. New York: Twayne, 1996.

Roudané, Matthew C, ed. *Approaches to Teaching Miller's Death of a Salesman*. New York: Modern Languages Association, 1995.

Roudané, Matthew C, ed. *Conversations with Arthur Miller*. Jackson: University of Mississippi Press, 1987.

Singh, Pramila. *Arthur Miller and His Plays: A Critical Study*. New Delhi: Deep and Deep Publications, 1990.

Smith, Leonard. *The Crucible by Arthur Miller*. Basingstoke: Macmillan, 1986.

Spaulding, Peter. *Death of a Salesman by Arthur Miller*. Basingstoke: Macmillan, 1987.

Spears, Timothy B. *100 Years on the Road: The Traveling Salesman in American Culture*. New Haven, Conn.: Yale University Press, 1995.

Spindler, Michael. *American Literature and Social Change: William Dean Howells to Arthur Miller*. London: Macmillan, 1983.

Wertheim, Albert. *Staging the War: American Drama and World War II*. Bloomington: Indiana University Press, 2004.

White, Sidney H. *The Merrill Guide to Arthur Miller*. Columbus, Ohio: Merrill, 1970.

SCHOLARS, STUDENTS, PROFESSORS

Abbotson, Susan C. W. *Student Companion to Arthur Miller*. Westport, Conn.: Greenwood Press, 2000.

Adam, Julie. *Versions of Heroism in Modern American Drama: Redefinition by Miller, Williams, O'Neill and Anderson*. New York: St. Martin's Press, 1991.

Bhaskara, Panikkar N. *Individual Morality and Social Happiness in Arthur Miller*. Atlantic Highlands, N.J.: Humanities Press, 1982.

Bhatia, Santosh K. *Arthur Miller: Social Drama as Tragedy*. New Delhi: Arnold-Heinemann, 1985.

Bigsby, Christopher. *The Cambridge Companion to Arthur Miller*. New York: Cambridge University Press, 1997.

_____. *Arthur Miller: A Critical Study*. New York: Cambridge University Press, 2005.

_____. *Arthur Miller*. Cambridge, Mass.: Harvard University Press, 2009.

Brashear, William R. *The Gorgon's Head: A Study in Tragedy and Despair*. Athens: University of Georgia Press, 1977.

Brown, John Mason. *Dramatis Personae*. New York: Viking, 1963.

Carson, Neil. *Arthur Miller*. Modern Dramatists. Second Edition. London: Palgrave Macmillan, 2008.

Centola, Steven, ed. *The Achievement of Arthur Miller: New Essays*. Dallas, Tex.: Contemporary Research Press, 1995.

Centola, Steven, ed. *Echoes Down the Corridor: Collected Essays, 1944–2000*. New York: Viking, 2000.

Corrigan, Robert W., ed. *Arthur Miller: A Collection of Critical Essays*. Englewood Cliffs, N.J.: Prentice-Hall, 1969.

Davis, Walter A. *Get the Guests: Psychoanalysis, Modern American Drama, and the Audience.* Madison: University of Wisconsin Press, 1994.

Demastes, William W., ed. *Realism and the American Tradition.* Tuscaloosa: University of Alabama Press, 1996.

Desafy-Grignard, Christiane. *Arthur Miller: La voix derangeante.* Paris: Belin, 2001.

Dunkleberger, Amy. *A Student's Guide to Arthur Miller.* Berkeley Heights, N.J.: Enslow Publishers, 2005.

Dusenbury, Winifred L. *The Theme of Loneliness in Modern American Drama.* Gainesville: University of Florida Press, 1960.

Erickson, Leslie Goss. *Re-Visioning of the Heroic Journey in Postmodern Literature: Toni Morrison, Julia Alvarez, Arthur Miller, and American Beauty.* Lewiston, N.Y.: Edwin Mellen Press, 2006.

Evans, Richard I. *Psychology and Arthur Miller.* New York: Dutton, 1969.

Falb, Lewis W. *American Drama in Paris, 1945–1970.* Chapel Hill: University of North Carolina Press, 1973.

Ferres, John H., ed. *Twentieth Century Interpretations of The Crucible: A Collection of Critical Essays.* Englewood Cliffs, N.J.: Prentice-Hall, 1972.

Foulkes, Peter A. *Literature and Propaganda.* London: Methuen, 1983.

Freedman, Morris. *American Drama in Social Context.* Carbondale: Southern Illinois University Press, 1971.

Furst, Lilian R. *Idioms of Distress: Psychosomatic Disorders in Medical and Imaginative Literature.* Albany: State University of New York Press, 2003.

Ganz, Arthur F. *Realms of the Self: Variations on a Theme in Modern Drama.* New York: New York University Press, 1980.

Graubard, Mark. *Witchcraft and Witchhunts Past and Present: The Blame Complex in Action.* Rockville, Md.: Kabel, 1989.

Greenfield, Thomas A. *Work and the Work Ethic in American Drama 1920–1970.* Columbia: University of Missouri Press, 1982.

Hadomi, Leah. *The Homecoming Theme in Modern Drama: The Return of the Prodigal: "Guilt to Be on Your Side."* Lewiston, N.Y.: Edwin Mellen, 1992.

Harap, Louis. *Dramatic Encounters: The Jewish Presence in Twentieth-Century Drama, Poetry, and Humor and the Black-Jewish Literary Relationship.* Westport, Conn.: Greenwood Press, 1987.

Harshbarger, Karl. *The Burning Jungle: An Analysis of Arthur Miller's Death of a Salesman*. Washington, D.C.: University Press of America, 1978.

Hayashi, Tetsumaro. *An Index to Arthur Miller Criticism, 1930–67*. Metuchen, N.J.: Scarecrow Press, 1976.

——————. *Arthur Miller and Tennessee Williams: Research Opportunities and Dissertations Abstracts*. Jefferson, N.C.: McFarland, 1983.

Hayman, Ronald. *Arthur Miller*. London: Heinemann, 1970.

Hughes, Catharine. *Plays, Politics, and Polemics*. New York: Drama Book Specialists, 1973.

Isser, Edward R. *Stages of Annihilation: Theatrical Representations of the Holocaust*. Madison, N.J.: Fairleigh Dickinson University Press, 1997.

Johnson, Claudia D., and Vernon E. Johnson. *Understanding The Crucible: A Student Casebook to Issues, Sources, and Historical Documents*. Westport, Conn.: Greenwood Press, 1998.

Jordan-Finneran, Ryder. *Individuation and the Power of Evil on the Nature of the Human Psyche: Studies in C. G. Jung, Arthur Miller, and William Shakespeare*. Lewiston, N.Y.: Edwin Mellen, 2006.

Kauffmann, Stanley. *Persons of the Drama: Theater Criticism and Comment*. New York: Harper & Row, 1976.

Kolin, Philip C., ed. *American Playwrights Since 1945: A Guide to Scholarship, Criticism, and Performance*. Westport, Conn.: Greenwood Press, 1989.

Koon, Helena Wickham, ed. *Twentieth Century Interpretations of Death of a Salesman: A Collection of Critical Essays*. Englewood Cliffs, N.J.: Prentice-Hall, 1983.

Levin, David. *In Defense of Historical Literature: Essays on American History, Autobiography, Drama, and Fiction*. New York: Hill and Wang, 1967.

Lima, Robert. *Stages of Evil: Occultism in Western Theater and Drama*. Lexington: University Press of Kentucky, 2005.

Mander, John. *The Writer and Commitment*. London: Secker and Warburg, 1961.

Manocchio, Tony, and William Petett. *Families Under Stress: A Psychological Interpretation*. London: Routledge and Kegan Paul, 1975.

McConachie, Bruce. *American Theater in the Culture of the Cold War: Producing and Contesting Containment, 1947–1962*. Iowa City: University of Iowa Press, 2003.

Meserve, Walter J., ed. *The Merrill Studies in Death of a Salesman*. Columbus, Ohio: Merrill, 1972.

Miller, Arthur. "The Limited Hang-Out: The Dialogues of Richard Nixon as a Drama of the Antihero," *Harper's*, Volume 249, September 1974.

Murphy, Brenda, and Susan C. W. Abbotson. *Understanding Death of a Salesman: A Student Casebook to Issues, Sources, and Historical Documents*. Westport, Conn.: Greenwood Press, 1999.

Otten, Terry. *After Innocence: Visions of the Fall in Modern Literature*. Pittsburgh: University of Pittsburgh Press, 1982.

_____. *The Temptation of Innocence in the Dramas of Arthur Miller*. Columbia: University of Missouri Press, 2002.

Parker, Dorothy, ed. *Essays on Modern American Drama: Williams, Miller, Albee, and Shepard*. Toronto: University of Toronto Press, 1987.

Porter, Thomas E. *Myth and Modern American Drama*. Detroit: Wayne State University Press, 1969.

Rahy, Philip. *The Myth and the Powerhouse*. New York: Farrar, Straus & Giroux, 1965.

Rajakrishnan, V. *The Crucible and the Misty Tower: Morality and Aesthetics of Commitment in the Theatre of Arthur Miller*. Madras: Emerald, 1988.

Rama Murthy, V. *American Expressionistic Drama: Containing Analyses of Three Outstanding American Plays: O'Neill: The Hairy Ape; Tennessee Williams: The Glass Menagerie; Miller: Death of a Salesman*. Delhi: Doaba, 1970.

Rowe, Kenneth Thorpe. *A Theater in Your Head*. New York: Funk and Wagnalls, 1960.

Rustin, Margaret, and Michael Rustin. *Mirror to Nature: Drama, Psychoanalysis, and Society*. London: Karnac, 2002.

Sarotte, Georges-Michel. *Arthur Miller: Death of a Salesman*. Paris: Didier erudition, 2000.

Savran, David. *Cowboys, Communists, and Queers: The Politics of Masculinity in the Work of Arthur Miller and Tennessee Williams*. Minneapolis: University of Minnesota Press, 1992.

Schlueter, June, ed. *Feminist Rereadings of Modern American Drama*. Rutherford, N.J.: Fairleigh Dickinson University Press, 1989.

Schneider, Daniel E. *The Psychoanalyst and the Artist*. New York: Farrar, Straus, and Co., 1950.

Schroeder, Patricia R. *The Presence of the Past in Modern American Drama.* Rutherford, N.J.: Fairleigh Dickinson University Press, 1989.

Schwarz, Alfred. *From Büchner to Beckett: Dramatic Theory and the Modes of Tragic Drama.* Athens: Ohio University Press, 1978.

Siebold, Thomas, ed. *Readings on Arthur Miller.* Farmington Hills, Mich.: Greenhaven Press, 1997.

Sievers, W. David. *Freud on Broadway: A History of Psychoanalysis and the American Drama.* New York: Hermitage House, 1955.

Strout, Cushing. *The Veracious Imagination: Essays on American History, Literature, and Biography.* Middletown, Conn.: Wesleyan University Press, 1981.

Vogel, Dan. *Three Masks of American Tragedy.* Baton Rouge: Louisiana State University Press, 1974.

Weales, Gerald, ed. *Death of a Salesman: Text and Criticism.* New York: Viking, 1967.

_____. *The Crucible: Text and Criticism.* New York: Viking, 1971.

Wilson, Robert N. *The Writer as Social Seer.* Chapel Hill: University of North Carolina Press, 1979.

Zeinneddine, Nada. *Because It Is My Name: Problems of Identity Experienced by Women, Artists, and Breadwinners in the Plays of Henrik Ibsen, Tennessee Williams, and Arthur Miller.* Braunton, Devon: Merlin Books, 1991.

THEATERS, PRODUCERS

Bleiman, Barbara. *Arthur Miller.* London: English & Media Centre, 1993.

Brater, Enoch. *Arthur Miller's America: Theater and Culture in a Time of Change.* Ann Arbor, Mich.: University of Michigan Press, 2005.

_____. *Arthur Miller's Global Theater.* Ann Arbor: University of Michigan, 2007.

Corrigan, Robert W. *The Theatre in Search of a Fix.* New York: Delacorte, 1973.

Jensen, George H. *Arthur Miller: A Bibliographical Checklist.* Columbia, S.C.: Faust, 1976.

Jerz, Dennis G. *Technology in American Drama, 1920–1950: Soul and Society in the Age of the Machine.* Westport, Conn.: Greenwood Press, 2003.

Koorey, Stefani. *Arthur Miller's Life and Literature: An Annotated and Comprehensive Guide.* Lanham, Md.: Scarecrow, 2000.

Langteau, Paula T. *Miller and Middle America: Essays on Arthur Miller and the American Experience.* Lanham, Md.: University Press of America, 2007.

Marino, Stephen A., ed. *"The Salesman Has a Birthday": Essays Celebrating the Fiftieth Anniversary of Arthur Miller's Death of a Salesman.* Lanham, Md.: University Press of America, 2000.

Martin, Robert A., ed. *Arthur Miller: New Perspectives.* Englewood Cliffs, N.J.: Prentice-Hall, 1982.

Martine, James J., ed. *Critical Essays on Arthur Miller.* Boston: G. K. Hall & Company, 1979.

_____. *The Crucible: Politics, Property, and Pretense.* New York: Twayne, 1993.

Mason, Jeffrey D. *Stone Tower: The Political Theater of Arthur Miller.* Ann Arbor: University of Michigan Press, 2008.

Miller, Arthur. "The 'Salesman' Has a Birthday," *New York Times,* February 5, 1950.

_____. "A Modest Proposal for the Pacification of the Public Temper," *The Nation,* July 3, 1954.

_____. "Bridge to a Savage World," *Esquire,* Volume 50, October 1958.

_____. "My Wife Marilyn," *Life,* Volume 45, December 22, 1958.

_____. "Our Guilt for the World's Evil," *New York Times Magazine,* January 3, 1965.

_____. "Literature and Mass Communication," *World Theatre,* Volume 15, 1966.

_____. *Salesman in Beijing.* New York: Viking, 1984.

Murray, Edward. *The Cinematic Imagination: Writers and the Motion Pictures.* New York: Ungar, 1972.

Orr, John. *Tragic Drama and Modern Society: A Sociology of Dramatic Form from 1880 to the Present.* Second Edition. Basingstonke: Macmillan, 1989.

Scanlan, Tom. *Family, Drama, and American Dreams.* Westport, Conn.: Greenwood, 1978.

Schlueter, June, and James K. Flanagan. *Arthur Miller.* New York: Ungar, 1965, 1987.

Schlueter, June. *Dramatic Closure: Reading the End.* Madison, N.J.: Fairleigh Dickinson University Press, 1995.

Warshow, Robert. *The Immediate Experience.* New York: Doubleday, 1962.

Weales, Gerald. *American Drama Since World War II.* New York: Harcourt, Brace & World, 1962.

_____. *Miller, the Playwright.* Third Edition. London: Methuen, 1985.

Welland, Dennis. *Arthur Miller.* New York: Grove Press/Evergreen, 1961.

ACTORS, DIRECTORS, THEATER PROFESSIONALS

Adler, Thomas P. *American Drama, 1940–1960: A Critical History.* New York: Twayne, 1994.

Ali, Syed Mashkoor, ed. *Arthur Miller: Twentieth Century Legend.* Jaipur: Surabhi Publications, 2006.

Andersen, Richard. *Arthur Miller: Writers and Their Works.* New York: Benchmark Books, 2005.

Berkowitz, Gerald M. *American Drama of the Twentieth Century.* Harlow: Longman Group, 1992.

Bigsby, C. W. E. *Confrontation and Commitment: A Study of Contemporary American Drama 1959–66.* Columbia: University of Missouri Press, 1968.

_____. *A Critical Introduction to Twentieth-Century American Drama: Volume 2: Williams, Miller, Albee.* Cambridge: Cambridge University Press, 1985.

_____. *File on Miller.* London: Methuen 1987.

_____. *Modern American Drama, 1945–2000.* Cambridge: Cambridge University Press, 2001.

Bigsby, C. W. E., ed. *Arthur Miller and Company: Arthur Miller Talks About His Work in the Company of Actors, Designers, Directors, Reviewers, and Writers.* London: Methuen Drama and the Arthur Miller Centre for American Studies, 1990.

Centola, Steven, ed. *Arthur Miller in Conversation.* Dallas, Tex.: Northouse, 1993.

Centola, Steven, and Michelle Cirulli, eds. *The Critical Response to Arthur Miller.* Westport, Conn.: Praeger, 2006.

Clurman, Harold. *On Directing.* New York: Macmillan, 1972.

_____. *The Collected Works of Harold Clurman: Six Decades of Commentary on Theatre, Dance, Music, Film, Arts, and Letters.* Edited by

Marjorie Loggia and Glenn Young. New York: Applause Theatre Books, 1994.

Cohn, Ruby. *Dialogue in American Drama*. Bloomington: Indiana University Press, 1971.

Dukore, Bernard F. *Death of a Salesman and The Crucible: Text and Performance*. Basingstoke: Macmillan, 1989.

Ferres, John H. *Arthur Miller: A Reference Guide*. Boston: G. K. Hall, 1979.

Gardner, R. H. *The Splintered Stage*. New York: Macmillan, 1965.

Gassner, John. *Theatre in Our Time*. New York: Crown, 1954.

Goldstein, Laurence, ed. *Michigan Quarterly Review* (Volume XXXVII No. 4) *Special Issue: Arthur Miller*. Ann Arbor: University of Michigan Press, 1998.

Gottfried, Martin. *Arthur Miller: His Life and Work*. Cambridge, Mass.: Da Capo Press, 2004.

Hays, Peter L., with Kent Nicholson. *Arthur Miller's Death of a Salesman*. Modern Theatre Guides. New York: Continuum, 2008.

Heilman, Robert B. *The Iceman, the Arsonist, and the Troubled Agent: Tragedy and Melodrama on the Modern Stage*. Seattle: University of Washington Press, 1973.

Hogan, Robert. *Arthur Miller*. Pamphlets on American Writers. Minneapolis, : University of Minnesota Press, 1964.

Huftel, Sheila. *Arthur Miller: The Burning Glass*. New York: Citadel, 1965.

Leaska, Mitchell A. *The Voice of Tragedy*. New York: Robert Speller, 1963.

Lerner, Adrienne. *Suicide in Arthur Miller's Death of a Salesman*. Farmington Hills, Mich.: Greenhaven Press, 2008.

Lewis, Allan. *American Plays and Playwrights of the Contemporary Theatre*. Second Edition. New York: Crown, 1970.

Marino, Stephen A. *A Language Study of Arthur Miller's Plays: The Plays in the Colloquial*. Lewiston, N.Y.: Edwin Mellen, 2002.

Marino, Stephen, ed. *Arthur Miller Journal*, 1:1–3:2, 2006–2008. (The publication of The Arthur Miller Society)

Martin, Robert A., ed. *The Theater Essays of Arthur Miller*. Foreword by Arthur Miller. N.Y.: Viking Press, 1978.

Mielziner, Jo. *Designing for the Theater*. New York: Bramhall House, 1965.

Miller, Arthur. "The Plaster Masks," *Encore*, April 1946.

_____. "Tragedy and the Common Man," *New York Times*, February 27, 1949.

_____. "Arthur Miller on 'The Nature of Tragedy'," *New York Herald-Tribune*, March 27, 1949.

_____. "The American Theater," *Holiday*, January 1955.

_____. "The Family in Modern Drama," *Atlantic Monthly*, April 1956.

_____. "The Playwright and the Atomic World," *Colorado Quarterly*, Volume 5, Autumn 1956.

_____. "The Writer in America," *Mainstream*, July 1957.

_____. "The Shadows of the Gods," *Harper's*, August 1958.

_____. "The Bored and the Violent," *Harper's*, Volume 225, November 1962.

_____. "On Recognition," *Michigan Quarterly Review*, Volume 2, Autumn 1963.

_____. "The Role of P.E.N.," *Saturday Review*, Volume 49, June 4, 1966.

_____. "Contemporary Theater," *Michigan Quarterly Review*, Volume 6, Summer 1967.

_____. "Arthur Miller on *The Crucible*," *Audience*, Volume 2, July–August 1972.

_____. "Foreword," *Toward the Radical Center: A Karel Capek Reader* by Karel Capek. North Haven, Conn.: Catbird Press, 1990.

_____. *On Politics and the Art of Acting.* New York: Viking Press, 2001.

EDITIONS OF MILLER'S WORKS USED IN THIS BOOK

Kushner, Tony, ed. *Arthur Miller: Collected Plays 1944–1961.* New York: Library of America, 2006.

SOURCES CITED IN THIS BOOK

Listed below are citations for quotes shown in the text.

In many ways, Miller expressed his view that "art ought to be of use in changing society." See Arthur Miller. *Timebends: A Life.* New York: Penguin, 1995, p. 93.

Many critics, including Christopher Bigsby, stress that the power of Miller's drama emerges from his ability to turn "abstract issues into human dilemmas." See C.W.E. Bigsby. *A Critical Introduction to Twentieth-Century American Drama*. New York: Cambridge University Press, 1985, p. 161.

Writing in *The New York Times,* critic Brooks Atkinson proclaimed that the American theater had "acquired a genuine new talent." See Brooks Atkinson, "Arthur Miller's 'All My Sons' Introduces A New Talent to the Theatre," *New York Times,* February 9, 1947, p. X1.

Critic Harold Bloom views Keller as "an authentic American Everyman" in that he is "an ordinary man who wants to have a moderately good time, who wants his family never to suffer, and who lacks any real imagination beyond the immediate." See Harold Bloom, ed. *Arthur Miller*. New York: Chelsea House, 1987, p. 4.

Following the failures of his play *The Man Who Had All the Luck*, as well as his novel, *Focus*, Miller's outlook profoundly changed in the wake of *All My Sons*. This is made clear from his statement that it was "somewhat like pushing against a door which is suddenly opened that was always securely shut until then. For myself, the experience was invigorating. It suddenly seemed that the audience was a mass of blood relations, and I sensed a warmth in the world that had not been there before. It made it possible to dream of daring more and risking more." See Arthur Miller. *The Theatre Essays of Arthur Miller*. Revised and Expanded. Edited with Introductions by Robert A. Martin and Steven R. Centrola. New York: Viking, 1996, p. 135.

This sets off a series of illusory flashbacks (although the play's original director, Elia Kazan, referred to these as "daydreams" in which "Willy is justifying himself") in which Willy drifts away. See Brenda Murphy. *Miller: Death of a Salesman: Plays in Production*. New York: Cambridge University Press, 1995, p. 33.

Kazan saw Willy's tragedy as a modern-day conundrum in which the individual "is Always Anxious! Because he is between two opposite fatal pulls: to best his neighbor, his brother vs. to be loved by his brother.

These are mutually exclusive, an impossible contradiction. Inevitably it will end disastrously," as, of course, it does for Willy. See Brenda Murphy. *Miller: Death of a Salesman: Plays in Production.* New York: Cambridge University Press, 1995, p. 32.

As a result, Miller was given a one-month suspended sentence and fined $500. Insisting "I could not use the name of another person and bring trouble on him," Miller was unrepentant. See Sacvan Bercovitch, ed. *The Cambridge History of American Literature. Vol. VII: Prose Writing, 1940–1990.* New York: Cambridge University Press, 1999, pp. 31–32.

More importantly, it inspired his challenging of the idea of an "American Dream" built on materialism and conformity to conservative values. As Miller himself stated, "The American Dream is the largely unacknowledged screen in front of which all American writing plays itself out. Whoever is writing in the United States is using the American Dream as an ironical pole of his story. People elsewhere tend to accept, to a far greater degree anyway, that the conditions of life are hostile to man's pretensions." See Arthur Miller. *The Theatre Essays of Arthur Miller.* Revised and Expanded. Edited with Introductions by Robert A. Martin and Steven R. Centrola. New York: Viking, 1996, p. 420.

His belief that theater could "change the world" as a moral agent never wavered. In his finest works, he articulated a nation's failings and its strengths. For Miller, a playwright "is nothing without his audience. He is the one of the audience who happens to know how to speak." See Arthur Miller, "Theatre: 'We're Probably in an Art That Is — Not Dying'," *New York Times,* January 17, 1993, Section II, p. 5.

Awards

"AND THE WINNER IS . . ."

	PULITZER PRIZE	TONY AWARD	NY DRAMA CRITICS CIRCLE AWARD		
			Best American	Best Foreign	Best Play
1944	No Award	—	No Award		
1945	Mary Chase *Harvey*	—	Tennessee Williams *The Glass Menagerie*		
1946	Russel Crouse and Howard Lindsay *State of the Union*	—	No Award		
1947	No Award	**Arthur Miller** ***All My Sons***	**Arthur Miller** ***All My Sons***		
1948	Tennessee Williams *A Streetcar Named Desire*	Joshua Logan and Thomas Heggen *Mister Roberts*	Tennessee Williams *A Streetcar Named Desire*		
1949	**Arthur Miller** ***Death of a Salesman***	**Arthur Miller** ***Death of a Salesman***	**Arthur Miller** ***Death of a Salesman***		
1950	Richard Rodgers *South Pacific*	T. S. Eliot *The Cocktail Party*	Carson McCullers *A Member of the Wedding*		
1951	No Award	Tennessee Williams *The Rose Tattoo*	Sidney Kingsley *Darkness at Noon*		
1952	Joseph Kramm *The Shrike*	Jan de Hartog *The Fourposter*	John van Druten *I Am a Camera*		
1953	William Inge *Picnic*	**Arthur Miller** ***The Crucible***	William Inge *Picnic*		
1954	John Patrick *The Teahouse of the August Moon*	John Patrick *The Teahouse of the August Moon*	John Patrick *The Teahouse of the August Moon*		
1955	Tennessee Williams *Cat on a Hot Tin Roof*	Joseph Hayes *The Desperate Hours*	Tennessee Williams *Cat on a Hot Tin Roof*		
1956	Albert Hackett and Frances Goodrich *The Diary of Anne Frank*	Albert Hackett and Frances Goodrich *The Diary of Anne Frank*	Albert Hackett and Frances Goodrich *The Diary of Anne Frank*		

	PULITZER PRIZE	TONY AWARD	NY DRAMA CRITICS CIRCLE AWARD		
			Best American	Best Foreign	Best Play
1957	Eugene O'Neill *Long Day's Journey Into Night*	Eugene O'Neill *Long Day's Journey Into Night*	Eugene O'Neill *Long Day's Journey Into Night*		
1958	Ketti Frings *Look Homeward, Angel*	Dore Schary *Sunrise at Campobello*	Ketti Frings *Look Homeward, Angel*		
1959	Archibald Macleish *J.B.*	Archibald Macleish *J.B.*	Lorraine Hansberry *A Raisin in the Sun*		
1960	Jerry Bock, music Sheldon Harnick, lyrics Jerome Wiedman, book George Abbott, book *Fiorello!*	William Gibson *The Miracle Worker*	Lillian Hellman *Toys in the Attic*		
1961	Tad Mosel *All the Way Home*	Jean Anouilh *Beckett*	Tad Mosel *All the Way Home*		
1962	Frank Loesser and Abe Burrows *How to Succeed in Business Without Really Trying*	Robert Bolt *A Man for All Seasons*	Tennessee Williams *The Night of the Iguana*	Richard Bolt *A Man for All Seasons*	No Award
1963	No Award	Edward Albee *Who's Afraid of Virginia Woolf?*	Edward Albee *Who's Afraid of Virginia Woolf?*		
1964	No Award	John Osborne *Luther*	John Osborne *Luther*		
1965	Frank D. Gilroy *The Subject Was Roses*	Frank D. Gilroy *The Subject Was Roses*	Frank D. Gilroy *The Subject Was Roses*		
1966	No Award	Peter Weiss *Marat / Sade*	Peter Weiss *Marat / Sade*		
1967	Edward Albee *A Delicate Balance*	Harold Pinter *The Homecoming*	Harold Pinter *The Homecoming*		
1968	No Award	Tom Stoppard *Rosencrantz and Guildenstern Are Dead*	Tom Stoppard *Rosencrantz and Guildenstern Are Dead*		
1969	Howard Sackler *The Great White Hope*	Howard Sackler *The Great White Hope*	Howard Sackler *The Great White Hope*		
1970	Charles Gordone *No Place to Be Somebody*	Frank McMahon *Borstal Boy*	Paul Zindel *The Effect of Gamma Rays on Man-in-the-Moon Marigolds*	No Award	Frank McMahon *Borstal Boy*

	PULITZER PRIZE	TONY AWARD	NY DRAMA CRITICS CIRCLE AWARD		
			Best American	Best Foreign	Best Play
1971	Paul Zindel *The Effect of Gamma Rays on Man-in-the-Moon Marigolds*	Anthony Shaffer *Sleuth*	John Guare *The House of Blue Leaves*	No Award	David Storey *Home*
1972	No Award	David Rabe *Sticks and Bones*	No Award	Jean Genet *The Screens*	Jason Miller *That Championship Season*
1973	Jason Miller *That Championship Season*	Jason Miller *That Champion Season*	Lanford Wilson *The Hot L Baltimore*	No Award	David Storey *The Changing Room*
1974	No Award	Joseph A. Walker *The River Niger*	Miguel Pinero *Short Eyes*	No Award	David Storey *The Contractor*
1975	Edward Albee *Seascape*	Peter Shaffer *Equus*	Ed Bullins *The Taking of Miss Janie*	No Award	Peter Shaffer *Equus*
1976	Marvin Hamlisch, music Edward Kleban, lyrics Nicholas Dante, book James Kirkwood, book *A Chorus Line*	Tom Stoppard *Travesties*	David Rabe *Streamers*	No Award	Tom Stoppard *Travesties*
1977	Michael Cristofer *The Shadow Box*	Michael Cristofer *The Shadow Box*	David Mamet *American Buffalo*	No Award	Simon Gray *Otherwise Engaged*
1978	Donald L. Coburn *The Gin Game*	Hugh Leonard *Da*	Hugh Leonard *Da*		
1979	Sam Shepard *Buried Child*	Bernard Pomerance *The Elephant Man*	Bernard Pomerance *The Elephant Man*		
1980	Lanford Wilson *Talley's Folly*	Mark Medoff *Children of a Lesser God*	No Award	Harold Pinter *Betrayal*	Lanford Wilson *Talley's Folly*
1981	Beth Henley *Crimes of the Heart*	Peter Shaffer *Amadeus*	Beth Henley *Crimes of the Heart*	No Award	Athol Fugard *A Lesson from Aloes*
1982	Charles Fuller *A Soldier's Play*	David Edgar *The Life and Adventures of Nicholas Nickleby*	Charles Fuller *A Soldier's Play*	No Award	David Edgar *The Life and Adventures of Nicholas Nickleby*
1983	Marsha Norman *Night, Mother*	Harvey Fierstein *Torch Song Trilogy*	No Award	David Hare *Plenty*	Neil Simon *Brighton Beach Memoirs*

	PULITZER PRIZE	TONY AWARD	NY DRAMA CRITICS CIRCLE AWARD		
			Best American	Best Foreign	Best Play
1984	David Mamet *Glengarry Glen Ross*	Tom Stoppard *The Real Thing*	David Mamet *Glengarry Glen Ross*	No Award	Tom Stoppard *The Real Thing*
1985	Stephen Sondheim, music/lyrics James Lapine, book *Sunday in the Park with George*	Neil Simon *Biloxi Blues*	August Wilson *Ma Rainey's Black Bottom*		
1986	No Award	Herb Gardener *I'm Not Rappaport*	Michael Frayn *Benefactors*	No Award	Sam Shepard *A Lie of the Mind*
1987	August Wilson *Fences*	August Wilson *Fences*	No Award	Christopher Hampton *Les Liaisons Dangereuses*	August Wilson *Fences*
1988	Alfred Uhry *Driving Miss Daisy*	David Henry Hwang *M. Butterfly*	No Award	Athol Fugard *Road to Mecca*	August Wilson *Joe Turner's Come and Gone*
1989	Wendy Wasserstein *The Heidi Chronicles*	Wendy Wasserstein *The Heidi Chronicles*	No Award	Brian Friel *Aristocrats*	Wendy Wasserstein *The Heidi Chronicles*
1990	August Wilson *The Piano Lesson*	Frank Galati *The Grapes of Wrath*	No Award	Peter Nichols *Privates on Parade*	August Wilson *The Piano Lesson*
1991	Neil Simon *Lost in Yonkers*	Neil Simon *Lost in Yonkers*	No Award	Timberlake Wertenbaker *Our Country's Good*	John Guare *Six Degrees of Separation*
1992	Robert Schenkkan *The Kentucky Cycle*	Brian Friel *Dancing at Lughnasa*	August Wilson *Two Trains Running*	No Award	Brian Friel *Dancing at Lughnasa*
1993	Tony Kushner *Angels in America: Millennium Approaches*	Tony Kushner *Angels in America: Millennium Approaches*	No Award	Frank McGuinness *Someone Who'll Watch Over Me*	Tony Kushner *Angels in America: Millennium Approaches*
1994	Edward Albee *Three Tall Women*	Tony Kushner *Angels in America: Perestroika*	Edward Albee *Three Tall Women*		

	PULITZER PRIZE	TONY AWARD	NY DRAMA CRITICS CIRCLE AWARD		
			Best American	Best Foreign	Best Play
1995	Horton Foote *The Young Man From Atlanta*	Terrence McNally *Love! Valour! Compassion!*	Terrence McNally *Love! Valour! Compassion!*	No Award	Tom Stoppard *Arcadia*
1996	Jonathan Larson *Rent*	Terrence McNally *Master Class*	No Award	Brian Friel *Molly Sweeney*	August Wilson *Seven Guitars*
1997	No Award	Alfred Uhry *The Last Night of Ballyhoo*	No Award	David Hare *Skylight*	Paula Vogel *How I Learned to Drive*
1998	Paula Vogel *How I Learned to Drive*	Yasmina Reza *Art*	Tina Howe *Pride's Crossing*	No Award	Yasmina Reza *Art*
1999	Margaret Edson *Wit*	Warren Leight *Side Man*	No Award	Patrick Marber *Closer*	Margaret Edson *Wit*
2000	Donald Margulies *Dinner with Friends*	Michael Frayn *Copenhagen*	No Award	Michael Frayn *Copenhagen*	August Wilson *Jitney*
2001	David Auburn *Proof*	David Auburn *Proof*	David Auburn *Proof*	No Award	Tom Stoppard *The Invention of Love*
2002	Suzan-Lori Parks *Topdog/Underdog*	Edward Albee *The Goat: or, Who Is Sylvia?*	Edward Albee *The Goat: or, Who Is Sylvia?*		
2003	Nilo Cruz *Anna in the Tropics*	Richard Greenburg *Take Me Out*	No Award	Alan Bennett *Talking Heads*	Richard Greenburg *Take Me Out*
2004	Doug Wright *I Am My Own Wife*	Doug Wright *I Am My Own Wife*	Lynn Nottage *Intimate Apparel*		

INDEX

The entries in the index include highlights from the main In an Hour essay portion of the book.

ABOUT THE AUTHOR

James Fisher, professor of theatre and head of the Department of Theatre at the University of North Carolina at Greensboro, has authored several books, including *Understanding Tony Kushner* (University of South Carolina Press, 2008), *The Historical Dictionary of the American Theater: Modernism* (Scarecrow Press, 2007; co-authored with Felicia Hardison Londré), *The Theater of Tony Kushner: Living Past Hope* (NY: Routledge, 2001), *Eddie Cantor: A Bio-Bibliography* (Greenwood Press, 1997), *Spencer Tracy: A Bio-Bibliography* (Greenwood Press, 1994), *Al Jolson: A Bio-Bibliography* (Greenwood Press, 1994), and *The Theatre of Yesterday and Tomorrow: Commedia dell'Arte on the Modern Stage* (Edwin Mellen, 1992). He has edited *"We Will Be Citizens": New Essays on Gay and Lesbian Theater* (McFarland, 2008), six volumes of *The Puppetry Yearbook* (Edwin Mellen Press), and *Tony Kushner: New Essays on the Art and Politics of the Plays* (McFarland, 2006). He is also a director and actor, author of two plays (*The Bogus Bride* [1982] and *The Braggart Soldier*, freely adapted from Plautus's *Miles Gloriosus* [2006]), and served as book review editor for both the *Journal of Dramatic Theory and Criticism* (1989–2003) and *Broadside*, the publication of the Theatre Library Association (2005–2009). Fisher was McLain-McTurnan-Arnold Research Scholar at Wabash College in 1987–1988 and 1999–2000, where he taught for twenty-nine years, and was named "Theatre Person of the Year" by the Indiana Theatre Association in 1997. In 2007, Fisher received the Betty Jean Jones Award for Excellence in the Teaching of American Theatre from the American Theatre and Drama Society.

ACKNOWLEDGMENTS

The author would like to thank his colleagues at the University of North Carolina at Greensboro and, especially, his wife, Dana Warner Fisher, and his children, Daniel and Anna, for their love and support.

Smith and Kraus would like to thank The Wylie Agency LLC, whose enlightened permissions policy reflects an understanding that copyright law is intended to both protect the rights of creators of intellectual property as well as to encourage its use for the public good.

Know the playwright, love the play.

Open a new door to theater study, performance, and audience satisfaction with these Playwrights In an Hour titles.

ANCIENT GREEK

Aeschylus   Aristophanes   Euripides   Sophocles

RENAISSANCE

William Shakespeare

MODERN

Anton Chekhov   Noël Coward   Lorraine Hansberry
Henrik Ibsen   Arthur Miller   Molière   Eugene O'Neill
Arthur Schnitzler   George Bernard Shaw   August Strindberg
Frank Wedekind   Oscar Wilde   Thornton Wilder
Tennessee Williams

CONTEMPORARY

Edward Albee   Alan Ayckbourn   Samuel Beckett
Theresa Rebeck   Sarah Ruhl   Sam Shepard   Tom Stoppard
August Wilson

To purchase or for more information
visit our web site inanhourbooks.com